Social Work in Medical Care

by Zofia Butrym

Lecturer in Social Casework
London School of Economics
and Political Science

LONDON

ROUTLEDGE & KEGAN PAUL

NEW YORK: HUMANITIES PRESS

First published 1967
by Routledge & Kegan Paul Ltd
Broadway House, 68–74 Carter Lane
London E.C.4

Printed in Great Britain
by Willmer Brothers Limited
Birkenhead, Cheshire

SBN 7100 3951 4

General editor's introduction

THE LIBRARY OF SOCIAL WORK is designed to meet the needs of students following courses of training for social work. In recent years the number and kinds of training in Britain have increased in an unprecedented way. But there has been no corresponding increase in the supply of text-books to cover the growing differentiation of subject matter or to respond to the growing spirit of enthusiastic but critical enquiry into the range of subjects relevant to social work. The Library will consist of short texts designed to introduce the student to the main features of each topic of enquiry, to the significant theoretical contributions so far made to its understanding, and to some of the outstanding problems. Each volume will suggest ways in which the student might continue his work by further reading.

Medical social work is, as Zofia Butrym points out, one of the longest established branches of social work. Its special problems—concerned with illness and disability, and the establishment of working relationships with the medical profession, with its high social and scientific prestige—are also of interest to social work as a whole. In this book attention is given to the historical development and current work of the medical social worker in both hospital and local authority department, and the main issues of policy in each are discussed. Medical social work emerges from the author's description and analysis as a field of considerable interest and challenge.

This book is one of a series devoted to an exploration of

the different branches into which social work is commonly divided. Each branch poses special problems and demands, as Zofia Butrym demonstrates in relation to medical care, special knowledge. Yet the branches must also be related; they must be *branches* of something. This topic of the relationship between what are described as the 'specific' and 'generic' aspects of social work cannot be usefully discussed without a conceptual analysis and detailed knowledge of each branch. The author provides the former and gives a detailed portrayal of one important 'setting' in which social work is practised. The book also illustrates another common feature of the settings of social work; they are continuously changing. This is what makes the description of any setting difficult and absorbing.

NOEL TIMMS

Contents

1

The nature of medical social work

'Generic' and 'Specific'

Medical social work is one of the longest established branches of social work, dating back to the end of the last century. This does not, however, absolve it from justifying a continued existence, and defining its terms of reference in the light of current social problems and provision. The need for constant reappraisal is common to many types of human activity, but there are particular reasons why it is of particular importance in social work. One obvious reason lies in the many changes in our social structure, and the evolution of the various social services to meet them. Another stems from the need to clarify the confusion which has arisen in recent years over the relationship in social work between the 'generic' and the 'specialist' elements.

Historically, social work began as a series of separate activities established at different times and in differing ways in response to particular needs. This made it difficult for quite a long period to recognise that the work carried out in different social contexts concerned with different social needs, nevertheless had common elements. Various branches of social work, such as almoning (the name by which medical social work was known until recently), probation, child care and psychiatric social work, were thought of as separate professions rather than specialisations within one profession. Some of the more obvious disadvantages of this were the problems of communication between social workers in the different areas of service, and the failure on their part to influence public opinion and social policy because of their inability to speak with one voice, and to make cumulative use of their experience. On the other hand, it is also possible to argue that this emphasis on specialisation was a necessary stage in the development of social work, since the recognition of the 'generic', or shared, components depended on their prior identification by the separate groups. One can also see a certain degree of similarity between social work and some other professions, in particular medicine, the origins of which can be traced to the existence of the barber surgeons and the apothecaries —two groups which believed they had nothing in common.

In recent years there has been a steady growth of a 'generic' orientation among social workers which has helped to correct some of the worst by-products of separatism. It has made possible such developments as the Standing Conference of Social Work Organisations which many hope will prove the first step towards the formation of a united association of social workers in this country. The basic assumptions underlying this 'generic' orientation are that all social workers subscribe to certain common values, that much of the knowledge on which they draw is shared, and that they employ a fundamentally similar range of methods and techniques. This recognition of the common elements does not resolve in any way the issue of the relationship between the 'generic' and the 'specialist' components of social work. This issue is complicated by the fact that the two concepts 'generic' and 'specialist' are at different levels of abstraction and are, therefore, not easy to analyse side by side. The notion of 'generic' and 'in common' is more theoretical than that of 'specialist' which is predominantly concerned with practical reality. It is partly this difficulty which prompts some people to think of these two aspects as mutually exclusive, instead of as complementary and interdependent. Thus they run the risk of confusing 'generic' with something which is elementary or superficial. This is not to deny the very real difficulties inherent in the task of examining social work practice in its various contexts with a view to identifying those elements which are shared with other social workers and those which constitute a special feature of practice in a particular area of problem or need. It does, however, pinpoint the urgency and complexity of the task. Many social work writers have evaded it, and by concentrating on the common features exclusively have, by implication failed to give sufficient recognition to the influence upon social work practice of the particular auspices—legal, administrative, and other—under which it is carried out.

The author who has contributed most in this respect is the American medical social worker, Harriett M. Bartlett, and much of the following discussion reflects her influence. Her frames of reference for the analysis of social work practice in any given field (1961 a and b) provide a very useful basis for identifying both the nature of the demands made on the different social work specialisms and some of the requirements for meeting these. According to Bartlett, social work practice in any particular field consists of the application of the essential (i.e. the generic) elements of social work values, purpose, knowledge, sanctions and methods to the characteristics of that field. The complexity involved in differential use of these common elements is obvious when one considers the application of any one of them to the various fields of social work practice. For example, respect for the individual, which is the underlying value in all social work, entails different issues for the family caseworker in a voluntary agency helping a couple with a marital problem, and for a mental welfare officer arranging a compulsory admission to a hospital. The same is true of all the other 'generic' elements. The differences inherent in their practical application are determined by such factors as the functions of the particular agency employing social workers, the type of problem encountered, the resources available, and the extent to which social workers are empowered to draw on them. All these factors

3

constitute, what Bartlett calls, 'characteristics of the particular field'. According to her, these characteristics are composed of the following five categories: the problem or condition of central concern; the system of organised services; the body of knowledge, values and methods; the socio-cultural attitudes prevalent in society towards the field and the nature of the problems with which it is concerned; and the characteristic responses and behaviour of the people served (i.e. of the consumers of the service). Unlike the 'generic' elements which relate to social work itself, characteristics of the different fields have to do with the special features of the different contexts in which social workers operate. Thus, with regard to the medical field, they include the various sets of values in relation to health and illness, and to sick people, which exist in our society; medical and other relevant knowledge which is brought to bear on the discovery, treatment and prevention of illness; the various services, institutions and professions which make up the framework within which health is promoted and illness fought.

Bartlett's framework provides a helpful beginning for analysing the content of both 'generic' and 'specialist' elements and their relationship to each other. The author's use of the idea of 'field' to denote the area of specialist practice instead of that of 'setting' which appeared earlier in social work literature, is of more than semantic interest. It conveys a more dynamic view than 'setting' and provides a broader perspective, the value of which is clearly demonstrable in the realm of medical social work. This branch of social work practice was associated until recently almost exclusively with the hospital, and as a result those few medical social workers who were employed outside it were often viewed as on the fringe of medical social work. The concept of the 'field of health', on the other hand, clearly includes besides work in hospitals, practice in the community, in research, and wherever social work is used to promote health or counteract the effects of illness in any way. This extended concept allows, too, for ongoing changes, for a shifting of boundaries, and discourages the type of outlook which clings to the status quo.

The characteristics of medico-social work

Concern with illness. The central characteristic of medical social work is its direct concern with the social and emotional problems connected with illness and its medical treatment, and with any consequent adjustments in the lives of patients and their families. It follows from this that constant encounters with the problems of physical pain, mental anguish, various forms of mutilation, and death, are a major feature of the work. The experience of serious illness brings forcibly to the minds of patients and those who care for them the inevitability of death. The fact that anxieties in connection with this threat to existence are only seldom voiced explicitly does not mean that they are not manifest in various indirect ways (Williams, 1966). The ability to sense and to respond appropriately to these feelings of apprehension and fear is an essential qualification for being able to help sick people. This requires both an appreciation of the needs of this group to which both psychological and sociological knowledge offer an important contribution, and also a certain type of personality and a degree of maturity to enable the worker to contain the emotional stress inherent in trying to meet these particular needs. For a medical social worker a degree of success in coming to terms herself with the inevitability of death, and a capacity to tolerate both physical pain and depression, are quite indispensable.

The diagnosis, treatment, and prevention of illness depend on a large number and a wide range of different contributions and skills, as well as on complex machinery and laboratory equipment. The organisational framework which exists to support and co-ordinate these various services is usually large and often inflexible. Social work forms a small part of that whole and its function is frequently described as 'secondary' to the primary purpose of

5

the medical organisation. The concept of 'secondary function' like that of 'generic social work' needs to be clarified because it is open to different interpretations, and has led to confused thinking. It is true, of course, that all medical services, whether hospitals, or general practice, or local authority Health Departments, are primarily concerned with the promotion of health and the treatment of illness, and not with social welfare. On the other hand, the distinction between 'health' and 'welfare' is becoming artificial. The relevance of social and emotional factors in health and illness has been increasingly forced upon the medical profession, and the acknowledgment of this is the basis of the concept of 'whole person' medicine, which is in principle accepted by most doctors, albeit frequently without all its implications.

Relationship with doctors. The problem of collaboration between social work and medicine, therefore, does not lie in a basic incompatibility between their respective aims, but rather in the difference in emphasis, in priorities and in the means adopted to promote these priorities. Stating the issue in these terms does not minimise the very real points of difference and of actual and potential conflict which are inherent in a partnership between social workers and doctors. For historical, social and other reasons, the power vested in the medical profession is considerable and extends beyond the authority derived from its function. This has a direct bearing on the multi-disciplinary approach for which all the health services increasingly call. Instead of shared thinking and joint planning the 'teamwork' frequently takes the form of a vertical chain of command, the consultant or the medical officer of health passing his 'orders' down the line.

The social worker's position in this situation is further complicated because, in comparison with doctors and nurses, she is a late-comer to the field of health, and does not share in the heritage of tradition of that field. In addition, the social worker's expertise in the treatment and care of sick people is removed further from the clinical training and knowledge of the doctor than the expertise of his other non-medical colleagues, e.g. nurses and physiotherapists. In his contacts with the social worker the doctor tends to feel less secure in his position of leadership, and may feel tempted to deal with his insecurity by adopting an authoritarian role rather than by discussion and argument. Many doctors (and nurses) are reluctant to acknowledge that the social workers' contribution in the health field is based on specialist knowledge and particular skills acquired during training. They maintain instead that, given time and a sufficient interest in this sphere of activity, they themselves could have met their patients' psycho-social needs equally effectively. This apparent claim to omnipotence has, no doubt, psychological origins (Jaco, 1958 and Becker, 1963), but it is also partly derived from an inability to grasp the true nature of social work. Doctors share this difficulty with many others in our society, whose image of social workers is that of people with kind hearts, a fund of goodwill towards their fellow men, and level heads. A recent small study of doctors' attitudes towards medical social workers (Butrym, 1966 b) found that the majority of those who envisaged a university education for these workers, saw this in terms of a general widening of horizons and enrichment of personality, rather than in the direct relevance of the social sciences as a preparation for social work. This discovery is fully in keeping with the findings of the authors of *Portrait of Social Work* (Rodgers and Dixon, 1960).

One reason for this widespread failure to give due recognition to the academic content of social work stems from the absence in this work of proven generalisations, analogous to those available in medicine. This coupled with the universal applicability of many psychological and sociological findings and their ready availability for lay consumption in popular books and magazines, contributes further to the underestimation of knowledge possessed by social workers in these areas.

Social workers themselves cannot be fully absolved of responsibility for having contributed to the ignorance and confusion surrounding their functions, through an excessive humility about the worth of their cumulative experience and a reluctance to formulate conclusions from it. Medical social workers have also shown a tendency in the past to rely too heavily on medical leadership in matters belonging properly to their own professional jurisdiction, e.g. decisions concerning the choices of priorities with regard to work with different types of patient with different kinds of problem. One manifestation of this failure to emphasise sufficiently their separate professional identity, as well as one of the factors that have contributed towards it, has been an excessive dependence by many medical social workers on their membership of 'the team' without an accompanying clarity of thinking about the nature of that team and their own place in it. In one sense, no-one working in a multi-disciplinary setting can avoid belonging both to the wide team which is almost synonymous with the setting or institution itself, and to the various subgroups within it which meet over specific tasks. The conception of 'the team' on the part of many medical social workers has been narrower and more static, in that it had to do with their participation in the work of the various 'firms' to which they were attached through regular attendance at the different meetings, discussions, clinical conferences, etc., held by these 'firms'. The desire to have regular opportunities to meet the consultants in charge of these units and all the doctors working under them to discuss patients under current care and potential referrals, was both understandable and laudable. Yet some of its manifestations reflected an excessive need to be 'in' on everything without a due regard to either the reality of the medical situation or the priorities demanded by their own job. For example, many medical social workers were prepared to join their 'firms' ward rounds which were exclusively concerned with the technical aspects of treatment and in which they had no opportunity whatsoever to make a professional contribution.

Issues in communication. The criticism of some of the

notions of teamwork in the health field is not intended to underrate the importance of close collaboration between social workers and medical personnel. On the contrary, if social work with the sick, the disabled, and their families is to have meaning for the clients and be effective, it requires to be constantly related to the medical situation. Equally, good medical treatment is dependent on the doctor's continual awareness of his patients' social circumstances and of their feelings about these. This mutual dependence makes effective communication between doctors and medical social workers of vital importance. Consequently, the means by which this communication is established and maintained must be thoughtfully chosen and efficiently used. On the part of the medical social workers, an important factor in facilitating communication with doctors is an intelligent interest in, and a sound grasp of, the medical facts in each situation. This is far more difficult to achieve than is sometimes realised. It is one of the major challenges of medical social work to establish a healthy balance between the ability to appreciate the significance of the various medical data and the avoidance of an excessive preoccupation with the more technical aspects of medical diagnosis and treatment. Such a preoccupation, all the more likely in view of the fascination and appeal of medical knowledge to many lay people, must be avoided if the social work orientation on the part of medical social workers is not to be lost.

A further prerequisite for effective communication between medical social workers and doctors, is clarity about the social work role with regard to the patients and their families, coupled with a real conviction about its importance and worth. Whilst these requirements apply equally to social workers in other fields, their importance for medical social workers is made exceptional by their close association with the highly articulate and critical members of the medical profession whose challenges in this respect they are constantly called upon to meet.

There is another reason why medical social workers

should be able to convey their role clearly and acceptably. This is the absence in medical social work of a legal mandate for action comparable with the mandates, for instance, of probation and child care. In contrast to these, the only basis on which medical social work can exist is the recognition by doctors—to whom all sick people come initially for help—that social workers can make a valuable contribution towards both the assessment and the treatment of the problem. It is important to recognise the many advantages of this situation which, at its best, can ensure an appropriate selection of those who can derive most benefit from social work help, can make it more possible to limit the size of the caseload and thus ensure the quality of the service given, and can allow a greater degree of freedom for the actual practice of the casework method. It is equally important, however, not to overlook some of the stresses inherent for medical social workers in the constant need to justify their professional existence through demonstrating the value of their contribution in work with individual patients in a field where other people's contributions are much more easily recognised and frequently more dramatic in their effects. The ensuing insecurity can lead to competition with other colleagues by taking on a large number of activities, marginal to social work, thus ensuring that one is not only busy but also seen to be busy. This solution is in direct conflict with the social work role in the health field where, more than elsewhere, clients look to the social worker for an ability to keep calm and to listen, and to help them to discover their own solutions to their problems, in their own time.

Some of the contributing factors to difficulties in communication between medical social workers and doctors, stem basically from the problem of the 'two cultures'. A good deal has been written on the effects of scientific training on doctors which prevents their seeing patients in the context of their individual personalities, their families and the society of which they are members (Jaco, 1958; Becker et. al., 1963). Current criticisms of the inadequacy of medical education for the tasks inherent in a doctor's job are many and severe. The social worker's educational background is, on the other hand, in the realm of the 'humanities' with particular emphasis on the social sciences; it contains usually no exposure to the discipline of scientific thinking and all that it entails. This makes it difficult for social workers to understand and sympathise with the scientific viewpoint. The fact that medical social workers' reaction to their ignorance in this sphere usually takes the form of excessive awe before anything scientific, whilst, as already suggested, many doctors deal with their ignorance of the social sciences by denying it (or sometimes the existence of these sciences!), does nothing to minimise the problems of communication between them. On the contrary, the attitude of scepticism on the part of many doctors towards any theory or knowledge which cannot meet the rigorous tests of the natural sciences, imposes the responsibility upon medical social workers to take particular care in not making any claims which they are unable to substantiate. This, coupled with the equally important responsibility, to which reference has already been made, to promote a better understanding of social work and safeguard it against being conceived too narrowly, or in a distorted fashion, constitutes a major task.

The dilemma inherent in this situation can be seen in connection with the notion of the 'casework relationship'. Like all social workers, medical social workers operate to a large extent through the medium of their relationship with their clients. It is in and through this relationship that their understanding of the individual sick person's problem is gained, and meaningful help is given. In spite of the importance of this in their practice, medical social workers must be careful not to present themselves as experts in the use of relationship. If they did so, they would be immediately challenged on the implication which no good doctor could accept that such a skill is exclusively theirs.

Use of social resources. It is in connection with the use of social resources that there is, superficially, the least conflict between the medical social workers and doctors. There is a good deal of evidence to show that medical social workers are highly valued by medical staff and others in the health field for their knowledge of the various services which exist to meet patients' social needs, and for their ability to make these services available to sick people and their families. Paradoxically, it is the ready recognition on the part of their colleagues of this particular aspect of their work which creates many if not most problems in communication and collaboration between medical social workers and other health service staff. The reason why most medical social workers react so negatively to being described as people who arrange social services for patients, is that they see a serious oversimplification, if not a distortion, of their proper role implicit in such a description. There appear to be sound grounds for such a reaction. Many doctors and others in the health field, fail to appreciate the complexity of the process which is frequently entailed in bringing together a particular patient and a given social resource. For example, a middle-aged widow with two adolescent children who was referred to the medical social worker for help with the financing of her special diet, had not only to be helped to obtain the extra money from a voluntary fund, but also on a more continuous basis to use the money for herself and abstain from sharing the better food with her children. She needed to talk about her own deprived childhood and to acknowledge the influence this had on her fear of being a depriving mother to her own children; this was an integral part of the help she was receiving from the medical social worker. In this case the medical social worker was successful in conveying to the doctor concerned the purpose of maintaining contact with the patient whose problem on referral seemed relatively simple. In another instance, however, a paediatrician who referred the parents of a severely subnormal child for help over an institutional placement for the child, insisted that his job was to help the parents to accept the reality of their child's condition; the medical social worker's task was to find the right home for him. He failed to recognise that feelings about a situation and arrangements for dealing with it cannot be split into separate watertight compartments.

Medical social workers in their desire not to be too exclusively associated with practical arrangements of various kinds, may lose the opportunity inherent in many patients requiring an environmental service to demonstrate the range of knowledge and skills such needs require.

Social work skills and medical care. It has already been stated that the basic compatibility of aims between doctors and social workers is not in itself sufficient to prevent conflicts arising between them with regard to particular aims and the means of achieving these. Such conflicts stem not infrequently from different working methods adopted by the medical and the social work professions. The doctor's job as the expert in the realm of diagnosis and treatment of illness requires an approach which is definite and authoritative. He is the person who, in many respects, knows what is best for his patients, and it is his duty to convey this to them unequivocally. Social workers, on the other hand, are concerned with issues which are less cut-and-dried, and they deal with questions to which there is seldom a single right answer. Their emphasis is on helping the person to reach his own decision by enabling him to become aware of, and take into account, as many as possible of the relevant factors, and then assisting him to carry out this decision. This more permissive approach on the part of the medical social worker is not always easy for doctors to understand and accept. It may even appear to them to cut across what they are trying to do. For example, a doctor who is convinced of the importance to a patient of immediate hospitalisation may not take kindly to the medical social worker's inability to respond literally to his referral of that patient to be persuaded to come in without a delay. To him persuasion in good faith is an acceptable means of securing the aim which is of such an importance to the patient, and the medical social worker's rejection of that means raises doubts in his mind about her acceptance of the aim itself. As such referrals usually take place in the course of busy clinics, the atmosphere is not conducive to a calm discussion about ends and means!

Another cause for misunderstandings is inherent in the emphasis given in social casework to the value in most instances of helping people to express their feelings of sadness, apprehension and anger, rather than their spending a large proportion of inner resources in suppressing these emotions. This view is not always shared by medical and nursing staff. The fact that a patient who is outwardly calm and does not question any of their ministrations is in many ways 'easier' to treat, mitigates further against their acceptance of ventilation of feelings as a therapeutic device.

This discrepancy in outlook underlines once again the importance of not carrying out casework in isolation from the medical reality and its requirements. This does not mean that medical social workers should abandon their own professional values. On the contrary, flexibility is made possible only by the existence of a firm base of principles. Providing such a base exists, one of the major strengths of social work is the capacity for flexibility and adaptability which stems from emphasis on the individual nature of needs and the uniqueness of every human problem situation. For example, helping a patient who has had eye surgery to abstain from weeping which might endanger the success of his operation, is as much medical social work as enabling another patient to express the hostility derived from his enforced dependence on others. The content and conduct of social work contacts with sick people will be affected as much by such factors as the nature of the treatment they are undergoing and their current physical resilience, as by their individual personalities and their social circumstances. Conversely, there are circumstances where other realities besides the purely medical one, such as the emotional, familial or social factors in a patient's situation, carry greater importance. It is the medical social worker's responsibility to present and interpret these factors to the doctor so that the patient's overall welfare is not sacrificed to the purely physical aspect.

Although it is necessary to be cautious about any generalisations of this kind, it would seem on the whole that whenever purely medical considerations predominate social work activity must adapt itself as best as it can to these (which may sometimes mean refraining from seeing a patient altogether or for a time). Equally, when the relevance of the psycho-social factors is paramount, medical treatment and care should be geared accordingly. In most instances, however, both sets of factors are of a considerable importance, and it is these situations which usually provide the real test for the degree and the effectiveness of collaboration between doctors and medical social workers, calling as they do for mutual trust and respect, and for a willingness to both give and receive.

Knowledge and Orientation. Because the basic terms of reference of social work—concern with people's problems in social living—are so broad, it is important to avoid the risk of being 'jacks of all trades and masters of none'. Some degree of specialisation is, therefore, inevitable, and its extent and nature are largely determined by the types of problem which are most frequently encountered and the kind of mandate which social workers in a given field have for dealing with these problems. For medical social workers the main area of specialist knowledge is in the realm of the psychology and sociology of illness and those social institutions which are concerned with the prevention, treatment and containment of sickness.

Knowledge about the psycho-social needs of sick and disabled people is already quite extensive and is constantly growing. Both dynamic psychology and sociology are major sources of the social worker's understanding in this respect. What are the meaning and the implications of the sick role for the patient, his family, and the various groups and institutions in the community; what is the relationship between a person's earlier life experiences and his present reactions to illness and disability; what particular past experiences or cultural factors have a major bearing on a person's attitude towards illness and dependency? These are only some of the questions which medical social workers need to consider in trying to help sick people and their families.

Another important area of knowledge which, so far, has been relatively little explored, is that of the relationship between different kinds of illness and the different stages of the process of treatment and recovery from them, and the nature of the patient's psycho-social difficulties. What is already known about this, such as for instance the particular difficulties of the convalescent period, or the problems experienced as a result of a 'stroke' (Hartshorn, 1967 a & b), serves to highlight the extent of our ignorance. Medical social workers have an important contribution to make through formulating their experiences with individual patients, making appropriate generalisations, and sharing their findings with others. It must be said that, so far, their activities in this respect have been limited. The reasons for this most probably lie in the absence of a research tradition in social work, and in a tendency for social workers to expend their energies too exclusively on their day to day problems.

Medical knowledge, a degree of which medical social workers clearly require, raises difficult issues with regard to an appropriate selection of the relevant aspects. The need for medical social workers to be acquainted with medical concepts and terminology underlines an important feature of this particular specialism in social work, namely the extent to which its close association with medicine serves as a challenge and a stimulus.

It is an essential quality in medical social workers to be able to maintain the necessary balance between a capacity to identify or feel with sick people and at the same time to avoid the risk of denying their importance as individuals through over-identification and transference of their problems to oneself. This ability can no more be taken for granted than the equivalent capacity to meet the particular needs of delinquents or deprived children. It is, therefore, one of the main attributes which are looked for in selecting applicants for training in medical social work and, in the course of that training, much emphasis and effort is put into fostering and strengthening it.

In all our social services at the present time casework is the method most constantly used by social workers. It is, however, a method which makes use of a wide range of different techniques in response to the differential needs of people with various kinds of problems. Therefore, casework practice in the different fields of social work has certain characteristics which distinguish it from practice elsewhere. In the field of medical social work two examples of this distinction are a particular care in the use of interpretative techniques in working with seriously ill people, and dependence on a large number of non-verbal methods of communicating with patients who are either too ill to speak or who have lost the power of speech or hearing as a result of their illness (Lambrick, 1962). There must also be a number of various adaptations in casework method made by individual medical social workers in intuitive response to as yet unformulated patients' needs. There is no doubt that in addition to the use of casework there is ample room in medical social work for helping patients and families through group work, and also for various forms of activity aimed at mobilising the interest of the community in the needs of the sick and the disabled. So far little use of these methods has been made by medical social workers in this country, and this is true of many social workers in other fields. There are, however, indications that possible developments in these areas are already arousing interest.

Finally, the importance in medical social work of relationships with colleagues of different kinds has its conceptual implications too. No amount of expertise in casework will make up for inability to work alongside other people in the health field and communicate effectively with them. The chief prerequisites of such an ability have already been mentioned. It is important to emphasise, however, that the recognition that relationships with colleagues are of as much professional importance as those with clients, must not lead to the mistaken conclusion that medical social workers practise casework with doctors, nurses and other staff. Although certain common insights are used in understanding people wherever and whoever they are, the nature of the disciplined approach, entailed in any professional relationship, in contact with fellow workers in the medical field and colleagues elsewhere differs radically from that used in casework with people seeking social work help. The difference in the purpose of the relationship provides the basis for these distinctions.

Training for medical social work

The particular requirements of the health field on social work practice, discussed above, have clearly important educational implications. This fact was recognised early by the profession itself. Shortly after the first almoners were introduced to voluntary hospitals by the Charity Organisation Society, a specialised form of training was set up for new recruits. Since these early beginnings, there have been steady developments in education for medical social work taking into account new areas of knowledge as these became available, and utilising current formulations. Medical social work has been unique among the various branches of social work in being responsible for the training of entrants to the profession. For a number of years the training course of the Institute of Medical Social Workers (formerly the Institute of Almoners) had the reputation of providing the highest standard of professional education for social work in this country. This was due to a number of complementary factors: the insistence on a university social science qualification as a condition for entry to the Course; the high calibre of teachers; the rich content of what there was to teach, and the importance attached to supervised fieldwork as an integral part of the training. Until 1929 when the first Mental Health Course was set up at the London School of Economics, the Institute's Course, although outside a university, was in fact the only course of training in social work of a university standard.

In the 1950s responsibility for providing professional training for other groups of social workers besides the psychiatric social workers was accepted by the universities with the establishment of the first Applied Social Studies Courses. Most medical social workers, particularly those responsible for the Institute's educational policy, saw this as the beginnings of the realisation of their hopes that ultimately social work training would be carried out in the universities and that outside courses, such as that provided by their own professional association, would no longer be needed. The 'generic' nature of the new courses created some apprehension, however, lest the emphasis in teaching on the common factors in social work should result in too great a sacrifice of the specialist content. Their acceptance as qualifying people for medical social work was made conditional on the inclusion of a certain amount of such content in the syllabus as well as the students' second fieldwork placement in the medical setting. Although experience has shown that medical social workers trained on 'generic' courses are not less competent than their colleagues from specialised courses (i.e. The Institute of Medical Social Workers Course and the Course in Medical Social Work at Edinburgh University), the issue of how much 'generic' and how much specialist content to include in courses for education in social work and what the relationship between these should be, is by no means resolved. On the contrary, a number of developments have added to its topicality and its urgency.

These have highlighted the limitations inherent in professional education for social workers in that most courses of university type in this country are of only one year's duration. The expectations held of social workers trained at the universities or equivalent courses, are constantly rising. This is partly due to the increased recognition of the contribution social workers can make to the welfare of society, and more specifically, it is a by-product of the establishment of the two-year Certificate courses in social work, in Colleges of Further Education, providing training for work in the Health and Welfare Services. Alongside workers from these courses, there is also a growing demand in Local Authorities for social workers with a university education for appointments to senior or teaching posts. A less positive trend which may come about as a result of these developments leading to an increase in the demand for university trained social workers, is the lessening of the recognition that all newly qualified workers, however sound their educational background, need opportunities for continued learning and professional growth in their first posts. This puts the responsibility on their employers to provide such opportunities and not to expect them to function up to their full potentialities from the outset.

Another factor contributing to the problems of teachers of social workers is that of the constantly expanding knowledge relevant to the practice of social work and for which there is often no room in the syllabus of a one year course. The failure on the part of nearly all the courses to include teaching about the functioning of groups, and to provide the students with fieldwork experience in group work, is but one reflection of this problem. The relevance of such teaching and its increasing importance are widely acknowledged, but owing to the limitations imposed by time, the regretful decision usually taken is to concentrate on equipping students well in the practice of one method, i.e. casework, in the hope that this will make it possible for them to learn the other methods in the course of their working experience.

There is also the factor of the changing nature of many the university social science courses from which candidates for professional training in social work come. An increasing number of these courses no longer consider the preparation of their students for social work training as one of their functions, and, as a result, fail to include any fieldwork under their auspices, or teach social administration.

At this time of transition in both social work practice and education it is difficult to predict any major changes. A new development in education is the four-year degree course combining broad social science content with professional education in social work. Medical social work is usually one of the options on these courses, except where the absence of adequate fieldwork facilities prevents this. A number of universities are also starting one-year and two-year postgraduate courses which combine professional training with work for a higher degree. There are signs, too, that the seventeen-months courses for graduates in other subjects aiming to provide both teaching of social science content and training in child care or probation may extend to two years and thus become acceptable for the training of medical social workers.

All these developments pinpoint further the problems which face the one-year courses. One of the possible solutions these may adopt is to restrict their entry to those candidates who are a little older than most new graduates and who have had some experience of working in one of the social services, as has always been done in relation to the entrants for training in psychiatric social work.

Whatever the changes in education for social work, these must be in keeping with the developments in the field of practice. A partnership between the two is essential to the future of both. The recognition of this in the past has been greater in medical social work than elsewhere, but there are recent indications that there are still considerable problems in achieving a satisfactory understanding between the two (Moon and Slack, 1965). One must hope for the sake of the sick, the disabled, and their families, that these difficulties will be resolved in the future.

2
Medical social work in the hospital

Historical background

Until recently, hospitals provided the traditional setting for medical social workers and only a very small number worked elsewhere. This is understandable when one remembers that when medical social work first came into existence at the end of the last century, hospitals were almost the only social institutions concerned with the treatment of illness. Even in more recent years, for reasons which will be discussed more fully in the next chapter, opportunities for social work with the sick and the disabled in the wider community have been severely limited.

The first almoners were employed by voluntary hospitals to prevent the abuse of hospital facilities by patients whose needs were thought to be more appropriately met within the Poor Law system. Clearly there was a considerable difference between this role and that of helping patients and their families, which the almoners themselves (and the Charity Organisation Society who sponsored them) considered to be the justification for their existence. It constituted a major factor in the ambiguity of the position of medical social work in hospital treatment and care which has been a continuous feature of the history of the profession. Whilst some discrepancy between *ego*'s conception of his role and *alter*'s conception of it is inherent in the concept of a 'role', in the case of medical social work the degree of this has been rather extreme. In addition to the initial lack of agreement, a number of other factors contributed to the confusion at the time when medical social work began. For example, hospitals had no efficient system of administration. This meant that from the outset almoners were often expected to undertake responsibility for various functions, such as the organisation and maintenance of a medical records system, or the arrangement of transport, not because they had a particular contribution to make to these tasks, but because there was no one else in the hospital to carry them out. It also meant that their dependence on the goodwill of the medical and senior nursing staff was greater than would have been the case had there been, within the hospital structure, some provision for arbitration between the various vested interests which inevitably come into play in any complex organisation. As a result of this many almoners were ready to pay almost any price to obtain access to patients so that those with social problems could have the benefit of their help, and sometimes failed to see that help given in isolation from the medical treatment would have its various limitations.

All these factors contributed towards the lack of understanding of the specific contribution of social work towards the treatment and care of sick people, which has always been of such concern to medical social workers. It is nevertheless important not to view the pre-1948 period of the profession's history in an excessively negative light. Many medical social workers were successful in establishing effective and mutually satisfying working relationships with doctors in the units to which they were attached. This meant that the needs of the patients in these units were well met and that the value of social work in the treatment of hospital patients was demonstrated to all concerned. When one considers their isolation, the burden of the various demands made on their time for duties such as assessment of ability to pay towards the cost of hospital treatment and care, their considerable achievement is a reflection of the courage and determination of many of the early pioneers. Had it not been for their success in demonstrating against so many odds to both their clients and to a number of their hospital colleagues the value of social work to sick people and their families, the era of 'almoners' might well have come to an end with the advent of the National Health Service and the disappearance of assessment of financial means. The fact that instead medical social work was recognised as an integral part of the new Service from the outset, as is demonstrated by the special circular sent out by the Ministry of Health to all the Boards of Governors and Hospital Management Committees in September 1948, shows that the pre-1948 almoners had not failed in their roles as hospital social workers.

The National Health Service was viewed by almoners with considerable enthusiasm as a liberation from the previous burden of 'administrative' tasks for work which they saw as properly theirs. However understandable this reaction, it was a denial of reality in so so far as it assumed that all the ills of the past were due to these specific tasks. It is not surprising, therefore, that after a brief 'honeymoon' period almoners found themselves still faced with a considerable number of complex and intractable problems in relation to their position in the hospital service. One aspect of reality which soon became apparent was that no amount of official recognition of the value of medical social work by means of Ministry circulars or the pronouncements of a few highly placed individuals could ensure either the understanding of the nature of its contribution or willingness to make use of it on the part of those individual doctors and nurses who were in the position to make referrals. In addition to the ambiguity of the almoner's role as derived from the past, several other factors played an important part in the limited or inappropriate use which some medical staff made of medical social work. Some of these factors are related to problems and pressures experienced by the doctors themselves. As Professor Titmuss has pointed out (1956), the fairly sudden transition in medicine from being predominantly an 'art' to becoming a 'science', has not been without its difficulties for the medical profession. The emphasis on increasingly narrow specialisations, coupled with the fact that prestige and prospects for advancement depended on acquiring such a specialisation, has inevitably focused the interest of many doctors on the laboratory rather than on the patient as an individual with emotional and social as well as physiological needs. Curricula in most medical schools, in which the absence of dynamic psychology and sociology teaching was a notable feature, both reflected this emphasis and reinforced it. In addition to this, many hospital doctors, particularly in the 1950's experienced a great deal of frustration in relation to their future careers, owing to the number of senior registrars for whom there appeared to be insufficient consultant posts. This 'bottleneck', in the light of the present shortage of hospital specialists, is puzzling, but the problem was experienced as very real at the time, and it is worth remembering in this context the findings of the Willink Report (1955) that the country would soon be over-doctored. Most people seriously concerned about their own future and faced with a highly competitive situation, find it difficult to invest a great deal of emotional energy in the personal problems of others. The doctor needs a degree of such investment before he can make referrals to a medical social worker.

There were other frustrations, too, stemming from the overall financial problems which faced the National Health Service since its inception: outdated hospital buildings, lack of space in clinics and wards, waiting lists, large numbers of outpatients who had to be seen within the span of a morning or afternoon, and others. The effects of these on a doctor's ability to give his time and attention to the less obvious and pressing needs of his patients must not be underestimated, particularly when he knows that the recognition of these will inevitably result in more work for him either in the form of discussion with the medical social worker, or in the writing of letters and reports, and usually in both.

25

Another difficulty for medical social workers arose from the necessity to belong simultaneously to both the hospital and to the community outside. Expectations stemming from these two sources are by no means always compatible. There is a tendency for the community to view the hospital as an institution concerned with welfare as well as medical treatment. This may be justified, as we have seen, in so far as medical care cannot be effective without due regard to the sick person's social needs, but the *degree* of emphasis on medical treatment or on welfare needs is of great importance. Conflicts can arise, and on many occasions have arisen, over such matters as the discharge of patients. The hospital may consider many ready to leave even though provision for their social care in the community is lacking. Equally, the hospital's view of what should be provided by the community for its frail and disabled members, often at very short notice, is frequently utterly unrealistic and based on an extensively rigid distinction between medical treatment and social care. Medical social workers have usually borne the brunt of these conflicts, accused by their medical and nursing colleagues of insufficient appreciation of the urgency of the 'disposal' problems of patients no longer requiring a hospital bed, and bringing upon themselves the anger of the community social services for making unrealistic demands on behalf of the hospital. It is probably not far from the truth to suggest that, apart from the patients and their families, the medical social workers have been the group most directly and adversely affected by the tripartite system of the National Health Service with its separation of the hospitals from the community health and welfare services. The absence, until very recently, of trained social workers in the latter has been an additional source of difficulty, increasing the problems of communication and of ensuring continuity of care.

In spite of these difficulties, the last twenty years has seen a considerable development of medical social work as a professional service to the sick and their families. A number of different factors have contributed to this, in particular the increased ability of social workers to use relevant psychological and sociological knowledge, coupled with an improved understanding of casework method and, consequently, a greater assurance in its use. In addition, medical social workers, no less than their colleagues in other fields, have derived a considerable amount of support from the growing awareness of the features common to all social work and from the resulting decrease in feelings of isolation. In particular, the movement in social work during the last few years towards a unified profession with improved opportunities for communication between social workers in different fields has led to a great deal of sharing and education which has enabled the particular groups to look afresh at what they were doing and question some of their ways of working. A very important aspect of this interchange has been the realisation by all concerned that they were not alone in encountering difficulties and frustrations both within their own agencies and in their contacts with others.

Current issues

Shortage of medical social workers. For many years the demand for medical social workers by hospitals has been far in excess of supply, and the advertisement section of the *Journal of Medical Social Work* shows repeated but unsuccessful attempts to attract staff. The situation has become accentuated of late due to the growing demand for medical social workers by Local Authority Health and Welfare Departments as part of their plan to implement the recommendations of the Younghusband Committee (*Report of the Working Party on Social Workers in the Local Authority Health and Welfare Services*, 1959) and the legislation which followed it. Some of the demand for medical social work staff on the part of the hospitals undoubtedly stems from their recognition of the important contribution they can make to the total plan of medical treatment and care. Factors such as the inclusion of social records in the list of the eight primary documents recommended as 'the permanent constituents' of patients' case folders by the Standing Medical Advisory Committee in its report *The Standardisation of Hospital Medical Records* (Central Health Services Council, 1965) provides some evidence of this. On the other hand, it is also important to recognise that some of the demand reflects a lack of clarity about the exact nature of a medical social worker's contribution, and is based on a lack of realism with regard to the scarcity of trained social workers in all fields, including medical, and the consequent importance of an economic deployment of such workers. Hospitals have perhaps been slow to recognise these facts because they were the first public service to employ social workers and long had a monopoly over almoners. Such attitudes are often illustrated by more willingness to grant an additional establishment for a medical social worker than to allow the department of social work to employ an additional administrative assistant or secretary. Equally, the long struggles which many a head of a medical social work department had to endure before duties no longer thought appropriate for the department were transferred elsewhere, demonstrate the durability of the tendency to consider medical social workers the right people to do the various 'odd jobs' which no one else wished to do or which would require the appointment of separate personnel. Responsibility for ordering surgical appliances, payment of fares to patients in receipt of National Assistance allowance, and arranging treatment by district nurses for patients in their own homes, are examples of the kinds of duties which medical social workers have had difficulty in passing to administrative or other staff.

A very real problem which faces the hospital administrators and medical social workers is derived from the fact, discussed earlier, that a hospital cannot fulfil its function of providing medical treatment without giving due regard to the social needs of its patients. The range of these needs is very wide, and it is by no means always easy to distinguish between the relatively simple welfare needs which can be met without the intervention of a trained social worker and social problems which require professional assessment and skilled help. There are, however, needs at either extreme which can be identified without much doubt. It is in differentiating between the two that the hospital institution as a whole and medical social workers as the group within it most directly affected and with the most to contribute towards a proper policy in the matter, have failed so badly in the past. One of the most striking findings in the Moon Report (1965) was that a large proportion of the newly qualified medical social workers were spending between one-half and one-third of their time on work which both they and their heads of department did not consider to require professional training and which, in their opinion, could be carried out perfectly satisfactorily by an administrative or welfare assistant. This finding is a serious indictment of the policy makers who have allowed a misuse of manpower resources in a public service to a degree which no business organisation would tolerate.

The increasing need for hospitals to compete with the community health and welfare services, and others, for medical social work staff, coupled with the changing expectations of the medical social workers themselves as to the nature of their contribution, are likely to prove powerful stimuli for change. The fact that the organisation of social work services in the Local Authorities Health and Welfare Departments following the recommendations of the Younghusband Report and its implementation, is based on the recognition that social workers with different kinds of training can be deployed to meet the various needs of clients, is also bound to have important implications for hospital social work. In fact, in some hospitals a mixed staff, consisting of medical social workers, social workers who hold the Certificate in Social Work, and welfare assistants, already exist, and it seems both inevitable and proper that such arrangements should become widespread. The most important single obstacle to a rational deployment of social work resources on these lines, is the absence of sufficient agreement about the criteria which determine the varying degrees to which cases present complex problems, requiring an appropriate degree of experience and skill on the part of the social worker. The lack of such criteria constitutes a serious limitation to a proper 'job analysis' in social work, although the need for this is increasingly acute in all the fields of social work owing to the considerable expansion of this type of work in our society. It is difficult to believe that the cumulative experience of social workers does not contain enough material on the basis of which some differentials as to both the assessment of need and of appropriate social work help could be identified and made available to the field. It is hoped that the incentive provided by the practical necessity of allocating work to different kinds of worker, will result in some achievement on these lines before long.

Continued need for medical social work in hospitals. The present emphasis on community care together with the rapid developments in the social work services in Health and Welfare Departments of local authorities, has led a number of people to question the future need for medical social work in hospitals, or to see it in a very restricted role (Jefferys, 1965 a). One obvious problem arises from this point of view. It would seem that any forecasts about the distribution of medical social work between hospitals and the community services must take into account the distribution of the medical services themselves between these two areas, otherwise they would negate the essential nature of medical social work as an integral part of medical care. The future evolution of the National Health Service in this respect is by no means clear : will the tripartite system of the hospital service, public health, and general practice, all differently administered, remain; will it be abolished in the near future; or will it be modified, and if so, how far? If the latter (and most likely) possibility, materialises, one would expect a development of 'joint user' social work services between the hospitals and the community services, as already happens in the mental health field. This would have the dual advantage of ensuring a greater continuity of care in situations where this is desirable, and of giving the social worker an acknowledged place in both the hospital and the community.

The major flaw in arguments advocating that all medical social work should be carried out from a community base, is that under such a system social work activity would be divorced from agency function, the community medical social worker being a visitor to the hospital and not a member of the institution itself. Besides going against the increasing awareness in social work thinking of the dependence of social work on agency function, this approach seems also to ignore more specifically some of the realities concerning the impact of hospitalisation and all this entails, on patients and their families. Hospitals are, inevitably, isolated to some extent from the rest of the community, and constitute little worlds of their own arising from their 'transacting' in matters of life and death. This gives them a special place in the eyes of the community, which is not free from ambivalence. Equally, the hospitals' attitudes towards the community reflect their awareness of the seriousness of the task entrusted to them and of the inevitability of failure in a number of instances.

Modern hospitals are scientific institutions to a high degree. With the best will in the world on the part of doctors and nurses, the impersonal aspects of the investigation and treatment of illness predominate, and increase the patients' feelings of impotence and resulting fear. Most of the laboratory tests and techniques require precision of a high order, with no room for variation, and equally, the more potent the new drugs and injections, the more care must be taken to exclude mistakes of any kind, particularly those that may stem from human error. Various elements of control, therefore, assume an increasing importance, with an accompanying diminution of the areas in which the sick person can make choices. For much of the time he feels at the mercy of others without being able to evaluate their activities and to know whether his trust in them is justified or not. In such a system, the medical social worker, in virtue of her freedom from direct responsibility for medical treatment or nursing care, is often the only member of staff who can consistently exercise a corrective influence on these aspects of hospitalisation which, however inevitable, are a serious threat to the personal integrity of patients, and therefore to their psychological health.

It seems justified to assume that the process of hospitalisation itself is a situation of crisis to many people, in the sense in which Gerald Caplan uses the term (Parad, ed. 1965). In that case, the contribution which the medical social worker can make at this point of crisis in the patient's life, has value and implications which extend far beyond the sense of relief immediately derived by the patient. Many other, more specific, but not necessarily less traumatic, 'crisis situations' exist for patients and their families in the course of their encounter with the hospital. Besides the more obvious ones, stemming from the threat of actuality of death and mutilation, there are an increasing number of acute emotional problems caused by such dramatic developments in surgical and other techniques, as kidney transplantations and certain forms of heart surgery, to mention only two. There is a further problem which faces most patients, albeit in differing degrees, namely that of the need to contain their anxiety in the face of the uncertainties inherent in the diagnostic process. Psychologically, this period of uncertainty imposes a heavier burden on many people than even 'knowing the worst'. Central to the former is the impossibility of any adjustment, while most people succeed, particularly with help, to come to terms in some degree with the reality of the latter. For many patients, support from a medical social worker during the period of waiting and anticipation with elements of both hope and dread, is, whatever the ultimate medical verdict, an important condition of living through this phase without too much lasting damage to their personalities.

If one accepts the reality of these various stresses inherent in entering a hospital, then it becomes difficult to subscribe to any plans for the future development and deployment of medical social work which would exclude the hospital as one base for its operations. To acknowledge the importance of this is not, however, to deny that the nature of medical social work in hospitals in future may differ in many important respects from its current functions. One would, for instance, expect a larger proportion of the work to be concerned with acute and relatively short-term problems stemming from the kinds of crisis to which reference has just been made, and a considerable lessening in the activities aimed at providing help with long term rehabilitation, resettlement, and support, for which most of the necessary resources exist within the community. There are also likely to be various changes in the method of helping, reflecting developments in social work in general. These will include more use of the potentialities inherent in working with groups of patients and their relatives, and attempts at finding ways of making the hospital community as a whole more aware of its therapeutic role in the broad sense of the term. Medical social workers in the past have been slow to extend their functions in this way partly because they felt more confident in their role as caseworkers for which they had explicit training, and partly because their basically insecure position in the hospitals presented them with many real difficulties in relation to such a 'broadening out'. The current emphasis on both group work and community work, is unlikely to be without its influence in the hospital field, even though it may be difficult to see at present the exact form which these developments will take. What is more possible is to delineate, more specifically than has been attempted earlier, some of the types of problem which appear to fall clearly within the terms of reference of a hospital based medical social worker, and it seems appropriate that the concluding pages of this chapter should be concerned with this task.

Some medical social problems characteristic of the hospital field

Two general points need to be borne in mind when reading the case illustrations given below.

Firstly, the focus of the discussion of these situations is on the problems created by the given illness and its hospital treatment, and not on social work activity as such. Therefore, many important questions concerning the latter must remain unanswered.

Secondly, in all the cases described, there was regular and frequent communication between the medical social workers and the doctors, but this is not explicitly stated in all the accounts, because of the need to keep the illustrations as brief and concise as possible.

Loss, or threat of loss, of various kinds. Mrs. B. was 45 when the medical social worker first met her. She was admitted for the removal of her second breast due to cancer. Her first mastectomy had taken place two years previously at another hospital. She referred herself to the medical social worker by stopping her on the ward under the pretext of handing her a Hospital Savings Association voucher. She knew her diagnosis, and during this first contact and later she talked at great length about her fears of it, wondering repeatedly what she had done to deserve it. She felt particularly bitter because her illness came shortly after her remarriage, and she and her second husband had had so little time together free from this worry. She described her marriage as very happy, and presented her husband as someone who would not consider any alternative to looking after her himself on her return home from hospital. Mrs. B. was specifically worried about the disfigurement which would result from her operation. She found the prospect of this repulsive and cried freely at the thought of it. She derived considerable comfort from being able to share her worries with the medical social worker, and once the operation was over became much happier. She ceased to refer to her diagnosis and to its implications, but instead talked a great deal about her return home and future plans. She did not, however, wish the medical social worker to communicate with her husband, taking the line that he was fully in control of the situation.

The patient was readmitted six months later with a fracture of her hip caused by the spread of cancer to her bones. This time, she dealt with her distress by denying the seriousness of her medical condition: the fracture was simply 'a nuisance' which had necessitated re-admission to hospital. She could not, however, maintain this attitude consistently, and had spells of depression. She then focused her worry on such matters as the discomfort of the position in which she had to lie, her inability to read or shampoo her hair, and similar 'safe' topics. After several weeks in hospital, Mrs. B. insisted on returning home. She was discharged by the doctors in spite of the fact that her fracture had not healed, because it was felt that she would be happier at home, and the prospects of any improvement in her condition were thought to be very poor. Again she maintained that her husband was able to make all the necessary arrangements for her care and that there was no need for him to see the medical social worker. The worker's first contact with the husband came a few weeks after Mrs. B.'s discharge from hospital. He came to see her on his own initiative while the patient was being seen in the clinic. He was a good looking man, a good deal younger than the patient, who seemed near the end of his tether and in great need of help in his own right. He told the medical social worker that he had come without his wife's knowledge and that, if she knew of his visit, she would accuse him of 'plotting' against her. He described how unbearable his life was at home because of his wife's insistence that he did everything himself and her refusal of any help from outside. He was clearly not able to oppose his wife in any way and did not appear to expect anything from the medical social worker other than sympathy and support to enable him preserve his sanity for which he feared. He was seen on several subsequent occasions, and he seemed to be helped through the medical social worker's recognition of the great strain under which he found himself. Mrs. B. was also seen on a number of occasions during this period, including several home visits. On each one of these the medical social worker was impressed by the thoughtfulness and care which clearly underlay the arrangements made for her by the husband who was away working during the day time. The room in which Mrs. B. was lying was spotlessly clean, she was generally comfortable, and well provided for with hot thermos flasks, books, etc. She gave no overt recognition to the burden this imposed on him, but her continued and increasing emphasis on his enjoyment in doing things for her, seemed to indicate an underlying anxiety.

Mrs. B.'s next admission to hospital came a few months after her previous discharge and was made necessary by a fracture in her other leg. X-rays revealed widespread secondary cancer deposits in her bones, and further surgery had been decided upon as a last measure aimed at slowing down the spread of the disease and giving her some palliative help. She had been warned about the risks inherent in this particular procedure, particularly that of loss of sight, and expressed considerable anxiety on this score. At this time too she showed concern for her husband and talked of the unhappiness she had brought him through marrying him. She also spoke at some length about suffering, both in general terms and with regard to herself trying to find some purpose in it. Although she had no specific religious allegiance she was able to formulate a philosophy which brought her considerable relief.

The medical social worker continued to see the husband throughout this period. His former resentment towards his wife gave place to dejection and despair. He, too, introduced religion into his discussions with the worker. His belief in the existence of some supernatural power was more tentative than his wife's, but he showed a great need to feel that there was an ultimate answer to the inexplicable facets of life. He also clearly derived considerable comfort and relief from the fact that the medical social worker considered his struggles in this respect as valid and purposeful.

The operation was remarkably successful, and for a short time there followed such a considerable improvement in Mrs. B.'s condition that she was able to walk again for the first time in many months. She left the hospital and went to convalesce with a relative where she was very happy and completely free from pain.

She was readmitted after a few weeks, suffering from meningitis and dying. Following intensive drug therapy, the meningitis cleared up and she regained consciousness. However, X-rays showed that the disease was spreading very fast, and in spite of the temporary improvement, it was unmistakable that Mrs. B. was slowly dying. The medical social worker was now seeing her daily. Although she was depressed at times, particularly following visits from her family, she was peaceful and resigned for most of the time. She did not refer to her dying explicitly, but gave the medical social worker numerous indications of being aware of this fact and of having accepted it. She lost consciousness a day before she died.

Mr. B. was completely distraught on the death of his wife, like a distressed and helpless child. He was incapable of making the necessary funeral arrangements and the medical social worker had to help him with these. Her enabling him to carry out his duty towards his wife to the last, was of a considerable importance to Mr. B. and contributed towards his ultimate success in adjusting to her death.

This case has been described at some length because it illustrates so clearly the nature of the problems to both patients and their families stemming from their exposure to loss. In this situation, a considerable number of different losses were experienced by Mr. and Mrs. B. prior to the ultimate loss of life by the patient. They both suffered a loss of freedom as a result of her many hospital admissions and her restricted capacity for movement when at home. Both she and he were affected, in different ways, by the changes in her physique caused by her illness—her loss of breasts initially, then her premature ageing and emaciation. All these changes had a profound effect on their relationship to each other. Mrs. B., who had married a man a good deal younger than herself and in many ways dependent on her, felt threatened in her role of wife when their positions became reversed and she had become so dependent on him. This led her in turn to make unreasonable demands on him and to deny the difficulties this created for him in order to prove to herself that she was 'safe' in his affections. Equally, the need to assume new responsibilities in the marriage, coupled with the loss of some of the support he was receiving in it previously, entailed a difficult adjustment for Mr. B. in the face of which he felt victimised and resentful at times, and then guilty as a result of these feelings.

The problems for both Mr. and Mrs. B. were made greater by the length of Mrs. B.'s illness and its many fluctuations. This changing reality meant that they were continuously faced with demands for adaptation. Mrs. B.'s frequent swings from hope to despair and vice versa were particularly marked in response to fluctuations in her medical condition.

Although shortage of space does not allow an analysis of the helping activity of the medical social worker, the case demonstrates the extent to which she played an important part in supporting both Mr. and Mrs. B. throughout their ordeal and, quite likely, in preventing a breakdown in the relationship between them. An important feature to note in this context is the continuity of contact between the medical social worker and the couple over the whole period, and equally, the value in this situation of the medical social worker being an integral part of the hospital and thus in a position to know the significant medical factors throughout and to share the relevant social information with the doctors and nurses concerned.

Acceptance of the medical reality. Like the previous group of problems discussed, this covers a wide range of different situations. The fact that many, if not all, people who are sick have some difficulty in 'accepting the medical reality' becomes very clear if one remembers that the term 'reality' conveys a misleading notion of absolute objectivity. In practice all reality contains a strong subjective element. Whilst it is true that some realities are more painful and harder to come to terms with for most people than others, the exact extent and nature of their impact on any particular person will depend on the person's particular personality and life situation.

The following few illustrations are intended to show some of these individual factors which affect adjustments to illness, disability, treatment, and the new mode of life which is frequently made necessary.

Miss A., a middle-aged woman, was seen in hospital for investigation of a severe anaemia. She was found to have a large intra-uterine fibroid for which a hysterectomy was recommended. She was referred to the medical social worker because she had refused this treatment on the grounds of financial difficulties and fear of losing her job. In her contacts with the medical social worker it soon transpired that neither of these reasons represented Miss A.'s real difficulties. These lay in her being a basically insecure and guilty person who had never come to terms fully with the death of her mother a few years ago, and whose way of dealing with her dependency and grief was to keep busy through heavy manual work. The need, inherent in the medical recommendation, to abandon this solution for the time being and to allow herself instead to become considerably dependent on others, constituted a major psychological threat. Her ultimate consent to the operation was the result of both the medical social worker's gradual help over a period of several months to enable her to feel less threatened by the prospect (her experience of dependency on the medical social worker during this period was an important factor in this), and the deterioration in her physical condition which was forcing her to recognise that she could not go on much longer as she was. Once she was admitted, there were a number of occasions on which she felt panic-stricken, and she found it difficult to believe that the operation would be successful because the strong component of guilt in her personality led her to expect punishment. Even after the operation, she continued for some time to expect trouble of various kinds.

Miss T. was a young German girl who was admitted to hospital initially for investigations of an acute backache. She had a resident job as a domestic with a family to whom she came on a labour permit, and had no relatives and few friends in this country. She was referred to the medical social worker by the ward sister because she appeared unhappy. It seemed at first that her depression was mostly due to severe pain, the uncertainty of her future, and her loneliness. Gradually, however, as she came to know and trust the medical social worker, she told her of a number of facts in her life which put her difficulties in a different context. She talked first of all of her unhappy family life, of her rejection by her father who resented that she was not a son and who had maltreated her physically as well as psychologically. Her relationship with her mother had been happier, but also coloured by the father's hatred of her. She also revealed on a later occasion that she had been raped after the end of the war by a group of Russian soldiers. She brought herself to tell the medical social worker of this last trauma because, during one of the most difficult periods medically when she was having very painful tests and was finally told she required a major operation which carried the risk of leaving her chairbound if unsuccessful, she heard from her fiancé in Germany that he was marrying someone else. Her distress about this had led her to connect the young man's rejection with the fact that she had told him of her experience of sexual assault; it thus confirmed in her mind the underlying fear that she was irretrievably damaged as a woman and that no man would ever want to marry her. The cumulative effect of these experiences, of acute physical pain, and of the uncertain future with which she was faced, was a degree of depression and loss of will to live which, apart from the suffering it caused her, seriously endangered the success of the surgical treatment. Matters were made worse by the fact that, owing to the seriousness of the operation and the degree of risk entailed, it had been decided to transfer the patient to a different hospital where she could be operated on by the best specialist available in this field. This meant that by leaving the familiar surroundings of the ward Miss T. was to be deprived of the last vestiges of security in her life. Her despair on being told of the plan confirmed the medical social worker's apprehensions on her behalf. To make the move manageable for the patient, it was decided that the medical social worker would continue to keep in close touch with her in the hospital to which she was being transferred in spite of the long distance. The continued support by someone whom she had come to trust and rely upon, coupled with the successful outcome of the operation, enabled the patient to regain her psychological equilibrium gradually. As was to be expected in the circumstances, the convalescent period was fraught with difficulties because her past deprivations made it difficult for her to give up some of the gratifications of her reliance on others. Her fear of independence took the form of various psychogenic symptoms such as migraines and even mild phobias, but eventually her basically strong personality won through and she was able to resume and enjoy a normal life.

Mr. M., a man in his early 50s, was diagnosed as a case of advanced ankylosing spondylitis and advised by the orthopaedic surgeon to give up his employment as a butcher. He was referred to the medical social worker by the surgeon who was puzzled by Mr. M.'s reluctance to act upon this recommendation. In the course of the medical social worker's contacts with this man it became clear that, in

D

addition to the very real practical difficulties entailed in a change of occupation after nearly 40 years, there were also less tangible reasons for this. It was only as the medical social worker came to know Mr. M. and became aware of the strength of his underlying dependency and guilt feelings, and also learnt from him of his past history, that the true nature of his problem became clearer. His early childhood was spent in considerable poverty due to the economic depression and the fact that he lost his father when very young. His widowed mother had a hard struggle in providing for him, and he described her as a 'wonderful woman' utterly devoted to him, her only child. She was determined to ensure an economically secure future for him, and at the age of fourteen arranged for him to be apprenticed to a butcher. This occupation, far from being Mr. M.'s choice, filled him initially with strong feelings of physical repulsion, and he described feeling sick at the sight of 'all this raw meat'. He was not able, however, to go against his mother's wishes, and after an initial period of misery and resentment, got used to the job. It seemed as if being settled and successful in this type of work became associated for Mr. M. with being a good son and making up to his mother for what she did for him. Consequently, whenever he contemplated taking any serious steps to abandon butchering, he became overcome with guilt and even panic. It was only as he was able, through his contacts with the medical social worker, to relive some of these feelings and develop a stronger grip on reality, that it became possible for him to consider the issue of future employment in its own right. The medical social worker with whom he had developed a very meaningful relationship, had for a time become a mother substitute whose 'permission' to change his work had enabled him to give up his former employment without feeling a traitor.

Two major interrelated themes seem implicit in these examples of patients' difficulties in coming to terms with some aspect of the reality imposed upon them by their illness. One is the influence of the previous adjustment by the person to his life situation, both in terms of its efficacy and the degree to which it is threatened by illness and its requirements. The other is concerned with the effects of dependency on different individuals, because enforced dependency is a feature of all illness, and in particular of hospitalisation. Most people have strong ambivalent feelings about dependency which are derived from their experience of dependency in childhood. Those for whom dependency is primarily associated with satisfactions and security, find the need to put themselves at the mercy of others relatively (but not absolutely) easy. Those, on the other hand, who have experienced severe deprivations, may need to go to considerable lengths to avoid the pain and suffering which being dependent implies for them, and will fiercely assert their independence. Many others, however, whose dependency needs were not satisfactorily met in the past, have had sufficient positive experiences to enable them to utilise later opportunities for making up for the earlier situation. All these different needs of hospital patients call for a sensitive appraisal and for an appropriate ensuing response. In some situations this may be the major condition for a patient being able to enter hospital at all, or to stay in it long enough to receive the necessary treatment; but where the problems are less acute, such an informed individualised approach is an essential factor in making the patient's encounter with the hospital a truly therapeutic experience.

Illness as a symptom of personal malfunctioning. All illness is psycho-somatic in the sense that mind and body interact and that, consequently, mental worry may affect bodily functioning and physical ill health the total personality. The term 'psycho-somatic' can also be used in a more restricted sense to denote a psychological origin to physical symptoms and pathology. This narrowing of the definition is useful in pinpointing those situations where psycho-genic factors are particularly significant, providing it does not underrate unduly the somatic elements. For instance, to say duodenal ulcers belong to the group of psycho-somatic diseases, is to acknowledge that certain internal conflicts may play an important part in their causation, but it is also to recognise that people whose psychological problems lead them to develop ulcers are in some way physiologically predisposed to them. Equally, to view the aetiology of illegitimate pregnancies exclusively in terms of intra-psychic conflict, is to deny the relevance of a number of other factors such as the cultural attitudes prevailing in a given society or a particular sub-group within it, towards unmarried motherhood, birth control, and pre-marital sexual relations.

As already suggested, however, the positive value of the 'psycho-somatic' concept lies in its providing an additional dimension to the understanding of illness and of the needs of sick people, and thus also to helping them. The following case provides a useful illustration of this.

James, an adolescent, was admitted to the orthopaedic ward of the hospital with a bad fracture of his knee as a result of a motor cycling accident. He was physically underdeveloped for his age, looked younger than he was, and seemed generally immature. He was referred to the medical social worker initially for help with his future work plans: he had only recently left school and was not yet settled in any employment. He had several short-lived casual jobs. Motor cycling was his craze, and he was a member of a small gang of boys who seemed to spend most of their time on their 'machines'. As the medical social worker talked to James and began learning about his attitudes towards various aspects of his life, she became increasingly convinced that she was faced with a 'pre-delinquent', i.e. someone whose behaviour would have led him to appear in court had he not had this accident instead. For example, the motor-cycle on which this boy was riding when he had the accident, was of a class he was not allowed to use at his age. She was also able gradually to identify some of the factors which were pertinent to the situation. James came from a large family of brothers and sisters of whom he was the youngest. His father and brothers were all tall and physically strong men, in 'tough jobs', in relation to whom James felt clearly inferior. His mother had been going out to work for some years and although he spoke warmly of her, the medical social worker had gained a definite impression that in some respects the boy had lacked adequate mothering. In the light of all these factors, it looked as if James's inability to settle in a job and his wild motor cycling were reflections of a basic insecurity and a resulting need to 'prove himself' somehow. His prolonged stay in hospital and his contacts with the medical social worker provided in the circumstances an opportunity for him to achieve this in a way which was healthier and more likely to be of a lasting value. His relationship with the medical social worker reflected clearly the nature and the development of these achievements. At first, it mostly met some of his previously unmet dependency needs and thus promoted the maturational process. It gradually changed into a relationship of a greater reciprocity and one in which James had the opportunity to learn a new social role—that of a young man *vis à vis* the opposite sex. Alongside the help which stemmed from his direct contacts with her, the medical social worker also enlisted other sources of help. Having ascertained that he was interested in technical drawings and that he seemed to have an ability in this direction, but was prevented from attending appropriate classes at the technical college because of his backwardness in arithmetic, she arranged for private tuition for him in that subject while in hospital. This proved an additional important gain since his very good relationship with his teacher provided James with the opportunity to model his own masculinity on other criteria than that of physical toughness for which he had neither the physique nor real interest.

It seems a fair assessment of the situation to say that his accident and his hospitalisation have provided James with opportunities for personal development which he might not have had otherwise, and that in that sense these events were a turning point in his life.

This is likely to be true of many more patients than is always recognised. Most important experiences in life provide people with some challenge and opportunity, and illness is no exception. To view illness as an isolated point in an individual's existence, without any connections with his past, or any consequences for his future, is to have a conception of human life which is based on a denial of its humanity. On the other hand, the recognition of the continuum of individual experience must result in an acknowledgement of the far reaching results of the right kind of intervention at the right time in the problem of a fellow human being. One of the most exciting features of medical social work in hospitals is that so many opportunities are open for this kind of intervention, and that due to the universality of illness those concerned represent a complete cross section of society.

3

Medical social work in the community

Historical background

Medical social workers (and other professionally trained social workers) have only recently been employed by Local Authorities: in the past these Authorities were concerned with the provision of personal services to very limited extent. From the time when the Poor Law system began breaking up, following the publication of the Reports of the Royal Commission on the English Poor Laws in 1909, until the outbreak of the Second World War, Local Authorities were faced with the considerable problem of the transfer and integration under their auspices of the various functions of the Poor Law. With very few exceptions, their energies were confined to this task; no new programmes were initiated which would put a greater emphasis on an individualised approach towards those who fell into the different categories of need. One exception was in relation to the ex-Poor Law Hospitals which were taken over in 1929, and some of which began employing almoners shortly after. Another area of Local Government activity in which medical social workers participated early were the tuberculosis dispensaries. Tuberculosis had been a notifiable disease since 1912, and Local Authorities were thus responsible for both the treatment of people who had the illness and for the prevention of its spreading. On the whole, however, the emphasis during the period 1909-1939 was on institutional care for the various 'problem groups' in society rather than on enabling their members to remain in the community.

The Second World War both gave rise to certain new social needs and highlighted existing problems, such as those of venereal disease, illegitimacy, and the various deficiencies of family life which were revealed in the course of evacuation. The contribution which social workers of all kinds could make in dealing with these difficulties was recognised, and as far as almoners were concerned the Ministry of Health exhorted Local Authorities to make use of these workers, particularly in connection with the problems of the rising incidence of tuberculosis, venereal disease, and unmarried motherhood. It is probably this emphasis on the special problems directly related to the social effects of the war which explains why there was so little spread of medical social work in the community during the first fifteen years following the end of the war. Apart from those in hospitals, nearly all the almoners who were in the employment of Local Authorities were in clinical settings such as tuberculosis clinics. Only a very small number were engaged in providing the other types of services which were made the responsibility of Local Authorities under the National Health Service Act, 1946, the National Health Service (Scotland) Act, 1947, and the National Assistance Act, 1948. According to the Report of the Working Party on Social Workers in the Local Authority Health and Welfare Services (1959), there were only fifty almoners working full time in all these services; another twenty worked part-time.

This Working Party was set up in 1955 to enquire into: 'the proper field of work and the recruitment and training of social workers at all levels in the local authorities' health and welfare services under the National Health Service and National Assistance Acts, and in particular whether there is a place for a general purpose social worker with an in-service training as a basic grade'. It was the result of the growing recognition that the needs of many people in the community who were at a disadvantage as a result of old age, infirmity, and ill health, were not being adequately met and that some definite and concerted remedial action was urgently called for. No detailed account of the Report of the Working Party is possible owing to the lack of space, but it contained a great deal of evidence on both the nature of the various needs and on the inadequacy of the existing social work services to meet them. Its major and most radical recommendation was that a new type of social worker was required to staff the health and welfare services adequately. These workers were to undergo a two year training, specially devised for their needs, at colleges of further education. It was thought that the provision of such courses outside the universities would ensure a larger number of entrants into local authorities' social work than would be feasible if recruitment were to depend entirely on university trained workers. This recommendation was also based on the Working Party's view that there was a wide range of needs among local authorities' clients the majority of which did not require the help of university trained and specialist social workers. The new workers with a general training in social work were seen by the Working Party as part of an integrated social work service which would also include two other kinds of worker. Firstly, another type of new worker, a 'welfare assistant', who would work under 'the direct supervision of trained social workers' and who would relieve the latter of 'a proportion of the simpler work and straightforward visiting'. Secondly, a number of 'professionally trained and experienced social workers to undertake casework in problems of special difficulty'. In addition, these workers were envisaged as 'advisers or consultants to other social workers in a range of services, and as supervisors (in the sense of teaching and guidance) of newly qualified or appointed social workers, and to assist with in-service training'. The Report envisaged their recruitment from family caseworkers, medical social workers and psychiatric social workers, and their specialist contribution was seen to relate to different work which was being undertaken in the different sections of the health and welfare services. The services to which medical social workers were thought to make a specialist contribution were those which concerned the needs of the physically handicapped, the elderly, and the sick in the community. The Report includes an exhortation to medical social workers, alongside their colleagues from the other two specialisations, to respond to the urgent need for their help in building up and developing social work in these services.

Current issues

Since the publication of this Report and the legislation implementing it, a number of medical social workers have moved from hospital posts to appointments in local authorities. These were mostly experienced workers many of whom had supervised students and had various administrative responsibilities in their hospital departments. As is to be expected in the light of the differences between local authorities and the pioneer nature of the majority of these appointments, there are considerable variations in the use made of these workers. Whilst the newness of the whole scheme precludes the possibility of drawing any firm conclusions, there are nevertheless a number of aspects worth considering, which concern the place of medical social work in the community.

Administrative considerations. The major consideration is the administrative framework within which medical social work is practised. At present, in many local authorities the services for which they are responsible under the National Assistance Acts and those which they provide under the National Health Service legislation, are administered by two different departments, namely the Welfare Department and the Public Health Department. In some local authorities, there is a joint Health and Welfare Department, whilst in some others the responsibilities for providing services to the handicapped laid down in the National Assistance Act have been transferred to the Health Department, leaving the

Welfare Department responsible for the other services under the Act, i.e. provision of residential accommodation for the elderly, the homeless, and other groups with similar needs. These administrative variations determine the local authority department within which medical social workers are employed. In many instances this is the Welfare Department, since much of its work is of such a kind that medical social workers can offer an obvious contribution. The opportunities for a specialist contribution to the work of the Department is a major attraction to these workers, as is the pioneering nature of much of the work. On the other hand, certain important drawbacks need to be acknowledged. The main ones are the absence of a tradition of trained social work in these departments which may manifest itself in various procedures and expectations which are not easy to reconcile with a professional approach, and the absence of a close link with the medical services. Examples of the former are such procedures as letters to clients being signed by the head of the department and not by individual workers, and insufficient recognition of the importance of confidentiality as reflected in arrangements for the keeping of records and in other ways. The latter factor has important implications for medical social workers whose emphasis is on a close integration of their own discipline with that of doctors.

Relations with public health workers. One might deduce from this that Public Health Departments are more appropriate places for medical social workers. There are, however, certain disadvantages in these too. Although in these departments professional traditions and ways of working are more firmly established, they are frequently based exclusively on the experience of public health doctors and nurses, i.e. health visitors. As already stated, only a very small number of medical social workers were found in these departments in the past, and those who were so employed most frequently worked in clinical settings such as tuberculosis clinics, and were thus outside the main stream of the department's public health work. As the community's need for social work became increasingly recognised, so medical officers of health increasingly saw the health visitor as a social worker as well as a health educator. Such an extension of her functions initially came about in part from necessity, owing to the lack of an alternative source of supply of social workers for employment in local authorities, but it had considerable advantages from the point of view of many medical officers of health. Health visitors were familiar colleagues with whom they had well established channels for collaboration and with whom communication was made easy by the fact that they had a relatively clear perception of each other's role. Social workers, on the other hand, were to a large extent an unknown quantity to both these groups of public health worker. The medical officers of health could not be as sure of their position with regard to them as they were in relation to health visitors. Even more than the hospital doctors they tended to react negatively to the concept of professional autonomy on the part of the social workers and feared, in consequence, the loss of control which employment of these workers in public health might entail. Equally, those health visitors who had come to see themselves as predominantly social workers resented, not unnaturally, the implication which the appointment of medical social workers carried that they were incapable of doing their jobs well and that the newcomers would be more effective. That some of these difficulties on the part of the health visitors in accepting medical social workers in the community stemmed from the ambiguity of their own position is shown by much of the recent literature about these workers and their changing functions (Jefferys, 1965 b). Equally, it is not unlikely that insecurity in relation to their proper role in the public health sphere led some medical social workers to reinforce the health visitors' apprehensions through failure to establish satisfactory communication with them. Whatever the additional difficulties caused by various extraneous or subjective factors between health visitors and medical social workers in identifying and accepting their separate professional roles in the public health field it is important to recognise that there are very real problems here, and that in a large part they stem from the lack of agreement about health visitors' functions to which reference has already been made. Although the Jamieson Committee on Health Visiting (H.M.S.O., 1956) supported the view that these workers were predominently health educators and not social workers, it also acknowledged that there was a large social component in health education of which they needed to be aware if they were to be effective in their work, and saw the giving of 'social advice' as an important function of health visitors. Difficulties are inherent in the different interpretations to which the terms 'social component' and 'social advice' lend themselves and it is not surprising that they have led to a good deal of confusion about health visitors' functions. Clearly, health education and medical social work are complementary activities (a fact which the Jamieson Committee had failed to recognise sufficiently by implying at one point in its Report that health visiting was the community equivalent to medical social work in hospitals), and because of this they are bound to overlap in certain areas. This calls for a close partnership between the workers in these two fields so that their respective expertise may be utilised to the utmost benefit of the community. Past difficulties in such collaboration were largely due to the lack of opportunity for health visitors and medical social workers to work side by side. Present opportunities for this, together with the attempt on the part of the health visiting profession to promote in their members a more positive identification with health education and to utilise their increased understanding of individual and social behaviour for making appropriate referrals to social workers, should have beneficial results for both groups.

The medical social worker and the general practitioner. Perhaps the greatest single anomaly about medical social work practice in the community under the present administrative system is that it is not linked with general medical practice. The failure to implement the National

Health Service Act of 1946 in respect of Health Centres has been an important factor; but, equally, the nature of the whole organisation of general practice and the system of payment of doctors, has prevented the attachment of medical social workers to general practitioners on any other than an experimental basis. Several such projects have been established however, usually either in connection with teaching, or with research, and the available accounts of these (Scott, 1956; Dongray, 1959 and 1962; Collins, 1965; Fairbairn, 1966) seem to indicate, as was to be expected, that the setting of general practice is in many ways very appropriate for medical social workers. This is because the problems which people bring to general practitioners frequently have strong medico-social components, and the clinical nature of general practice provides opportunities for intervening in these problems in a way which integrates the resources of medicine and social work. Various recent developments give reason to hope that future opportunities for closer collaboration between general practitioners and medical social workers will be more frequent. The trend on the part of many doctors to join in group practice and the incentives in the new system of pay for general practitioners to employ the help of other workers, are two important factors. In addition, there are indications of an increasing collaboration between local authorities and general practitioners in their areas. This takes the form of the local authority making available to the general practitioners both premises for surgeries and staff to assist them in their work. So far, in the majority of cases, the staff seconded have been health visitors and district nurses, but there does not seem to be any reason why in the future, when more medical social workers are available in the community, they too should not be 'loaned' in such a way. Such a partnership between local authorities and general practitioners would seem to be a very encouraging and effective way of minimising some of the disadvantages inherent in the separation of public health and general medical services under the National Health Service Act.

With regard to the present fragmentation of the social work services under different local authority departments, there is hope that this may become lessened in the not too distant future. Whilst the recommendations of the Seebohm Committee on local authority personal services cannot be foreseen, it seems nevertheless that these are likely to be in the direction of unification of some, if not of all, of the present local authority personal social services (*Social Work and the Community, Cmd. 3065, 1966*). Such a bringing together of the different services would have the advantage of opportunities for better planning and deployment of scarce resources, and the better career opportunities in a larger service might act as an incentive in the recruitment of new personnel. A possible danger is that of confusing the advantages of an administrative unification and rationalisation of services with the assumption that the needs of all clients in the new service can be met by 'all purpose' social workers. If such an assumption was made in the future concerning social work services of local authorities, this would ultimately lead to an overall lowering of standards. As already discussed in the first chapter, the concepts of 'generic' and 'specialist' in social work are complementary and not mutually exclusive. At their best, the re-organised social work services of the future could ensure a more effective use of the different kinds of social workers available, through their deployment in ways which would enable the best possible use of their various specialist contributions. A prerequisite of this is a better knowledge than is available at present of the range of the different problem situations which come under the auspices of community based social work and of the kinds of demands these make. The *Report of the Working Party on Social Workers in the Local Authority Health and Welfare Services (1959)* emphasised the importance of research of this nature, and it is to be hoped that this is given the priority it deserves by both central government and local authorities. Medical social workers in the community have clearly an important contribution to make to the task of clarifying the areas of work in which they have a particularly appropriate role to play. Because the community field is relatively new and unexplored in medical social work, it both provides scope and requires an attitude of exploration and experimentation on the part of medical social workers.

However difficult it is at present to be specific about the components of medical social work practice in local authority services, there are nevertheless certain areas of work which point clearly to its importance and which also suggest some of the salient features. Albeit tentatively, it seems worthwhile to consider some of these,

Some characteristics of medical social work in the community

Work with persons suffering from permanent disabilities. Such disabilities can be either static, as in the case of poliomyelitis and many congenital defects, or they can be progressive, as in the case of most cardiac and neurological diseases. Either type of situation presents many difficulties to the patient and his family, and whilst these are in many ways similar, there are also certain inherent differences. People with congenital handicaps have had to live with the realities of the condition and its limitations since birth, as have their next of kin. This means that they have reached some mode of adjustment a long time ago. This adjustment has usually followed a period of considerable distress and not infrequently a denial of the painful reality; the ultimate solution reached, therefore, tends to be somewhat rigid, inflexible, and generally precarious. For this reason, when adaptations of this original solution are made necessary, either by a change in the external circumstances, or because it can only be maintained at too great a price to the individual concerned and to others, considerable problems may arise. The following example illustrates the point.

Miss V. was forty when her mother died. She was a dwarf, severely disfigured, but capable of walking a fair amount, and of using her arms. Until her mother's death she had led an extremely sheltered life, had never worked, and hardly ever left her home. She was very self-conscious about her appearance and sensitive to other people's reactions to it. She had some unfortunate memories from her school years when other children teased and abused her. She was an intelligent woman who enjoyed reading and who had quite a sizeable library of books at home. While her mother was alive, her life of seclusion and isolation seemed to meet many of Miss V.'s needs although the ambivalent nature of her relationship with her mother and their frequent violent quarrels seemed to indicate a considerable degree of frustration. On the death of her mother, Miss V. became panic-stricken. She was afraid to be alone in the house but was equally frightened of the prospect of being with other people. Her despair and helplessness were pathetic. It was difficult for the Local Authority medical social worker to whom Miss V. had been referred by her neighbours to involve her in the discussion of any plans concerning her future. She had to begin by slowly building up a relationship with the patient in which Miss V. could find some support, and then gradually, as the patient's confidence in the worker and in herself increased, it became possible for her to summon the necessary resources for a more independent and active life. This readjustment enabled Miss V. to decide to enter a small Home for disabled people after she had experimented for some months with social contacts through attendance at a club and a day rehabilitation centre. She settled well and was both able to derive benefit and enjoyment for herself from her contacts with the other residents, and to contribute considerably towards their well-being.

In the case of patients who suffer from a progressive disability, many of their difficulties and those of their families, stem from the uncertainty surrounding the illness and the course it is likely to take. Constant emotional and material adjustments and readjustments have to be made as the medical condition fluctuates. At no point can these people feel that they have faced the worst, derive some comfort from this fact, and consolidate their achievements; on the contrary, every adjustment is accompanied by the knowledge that it may be invalidated at any moment by a deterioration (or a temporary improvement) in the patient's condition.

The case of Mrs. C. demonstrates some of the problems which patients with a progressive illness and their families have to face and cope with. She was in her early forties when the Local Authority medical social worker met her following a referral from the hospital where disseminated sclerosis was diagnosed. The family consisted of the patient, her husband, whose recent promotion within his firm had caused them to move to the area from a different part of the country where all their relatives and friends were, and three children aged 18, 16 and 4. Mrs. C.'s symptoms began soon after the birth of the youngest child, and when the medical social worker first met her, she was already considerably disabled although still quite mobile and able to do most of the housework. She knew the nature of her condition and that it would get progressively worse, and found relief in talking about it occasionally to the medical social worker as she was anxious not to burden her family. The worker was also able to help with the problem of the four-year-old son whose liveliness and need for contacts with other children could not be fully met within his home; as a result he was beginning to show early signs of maladjustment. A place was secured for him at a nursery school, and this proved very satisfactory. The medical social worker enabled Mrs. C. to express her discomfort and guilt at the fact that her two young daughters had to carry greater responsibilities in the home than would have been the case had she been well, and that her husband was deprived of a social life. In her contacts with the various members of the family, the medical social worker provided an important outlet for the feelings of sadness, frustration, and guilt which they were unable to share with the patient and which they badly needed to express rather than suppress. In the five years covered by the record of the medical social worker's contacts with the family, Mrs. C.'s condition underwent a steady deterioration, except for a few brief remissions. She lost the power of her legs, and the invalid tricycle which had been secured for her proved useless after a short time when strength in her arms failed. In addition, she lost her sight almost completely, and became incontinent. During the earlier stages of her illness, the services of a domestic help coupled with the family's own efforts enabled things to go on; but a time came when this was no longer adequate. At this point, Mrs. C.'s mother-in-law offered to come and run the house. This entailed a considerable adjustment to all the members of the family, Mrs. C. herself in particular. She found it very difficult to let her mother-in-law take over and was critical of her different standards of housekeeping and her attitudes towards the children. The mother-in-law, on the other hand, did not always appreciate the difficulties to Mrs. C. arising from the situation, and did not consult her sufficiently over matters in which she could and should have a say. At one stage relationships became so strained, in spite of the medical social worker's efforts to help both women in their respective roles, that the mother-in-law left. The break was not longstanding, however, and when the arrangement was resumed, both mother- and daughter-in-law were more understanding of each other and appreciated each other's strengths better. The next episode in this tragic story is likely to be that the family will have to face the need for residential care for Mrs. C. because any further deterioration in her present condition will make her continued stay at home impossible. How this decision is reached and implemented will be of vital importance to all concerned. The medical social worker's help at this crucial time may be decisive: the separation could be seen as something basically constructive, the result of a decision which has been reached after considered thought and full communication between them all, or as destructive, taking place in an atmosphere in which Mrs. C. feels unwanted and rejected, and her family feel guilty of a conspiracy against her.

One feature of medical social work in the community illustrated by both the cases described and which is likely to operate in many situations (including work with the elderly many of whom are likely to be among medical social workers' clients), is the much greater length of contacts than is usual in hospital work. Once a helping relationship with a sick or disabled person has been established, it is likely to continue for years rather than for weeks or months, and in many instances will continue as long as the patient lives. This fact would seem to have important and interesting implications for medical social work practice. Clearly, there are serious difficulties inherent in applying the same kind of thinking to the use of the casework relationship in long term contacts as in shorter ones. The former both impose a responsibility, and offer useful opportunities to medical social workers to give serious consideration to the time factor in the social work process. One of the reasons given for failure to attend to it in the past has been that hospitalisation and medical treatment within the institutional setting of a hospital imposed considerable external limitations on medical social workers in relation to both the length of time available for work with individual patients and the frequency of contacts with them. Whilst the adequacy of this excuse would seem to be open to serious doubt, it is clear that where no tangible, external time limits exist it is of crucial importance that some rational criteria should be devised to guide individual workers in their assessment of needs and in their approach to them. In a field where a case could remain current for twenty years or more, the justification for this kind of work should be considered. Otherwise chaos would result and the quantity of work would have inevitable precedence over its quality. Some social workers hold to a misconceived idea of equity which makes them try to spread their efforts equally among all the clients in their caseload, instead of concentrating their efforts where these are most needed and are likely to bring the greatest results at any particular time. The ability to do this is dependent on a degree of understanding of such timing factors as the frequency and the length of contacts at different moments in their client's lives. In her work with Mrs. C. and her family, there were long intervals during which the medical social worker was not in contact with them when things were fairly steady and no additional support or new adaptations were needed. At times of change and particular worry, she would visit daily, or even twice a day at times, if she thought that she was needed badly by both the patient and her family. An appropriate deployment of the time resource is an important and somewhat neglected aspect of social work theory and practice, and social work in the community is faced with a particularly acute challenge in this respect. If this can be met, a valuable contribution will have been made to social work everywhere.

Another important characteristic of medical social work in the community field which is also shown in both the cases, is that contact with patients usually takes place in their own homes rather than in the 'alien' setting of a hospital ward, outpatients' department, or clinic. This fact provides an important dimension for the medical social worker in her task of assessment which is less easily accessible to her hospital colleague. Seeing a sick or disabled person in their normal social environment, other things being equal, makes it easier to understand that person and to assess the impact of his illness or disability on his life. Yet, the opportunity to see patients in their own homes and in the context of their families, imposes certain demands on the knowledge and the diagnostic skills of the social worker which it would be a mistake to take for granted. This applies in particular to family dynamics which is much discussed in social work circles at present, but about which relatively little is known. Visiting clients in their own homes frequently entails seeing the various members of their families, both individually and as groups. The experience which the medical social worker can get of the family interaction can be invaluable in helping to understand the situation, and in effecting changes in the attitudes of the different individuals to each other, and to the sick or disabled person. Various kinds of collusion within a family, such as that between an adolescent daughter with a mild disability who fails to respond to efforts to find her suitable work and her depressed mother whose unhappy marriage is only made tolerable by her daughter's company in the home, can come to light much more easily and quickly in joint contacts of this kind than in individual interviews. However, direct involvement in family interaction on the part of the social worker makes heavy demands in both the diagnostic and the treatment areas. Since we have insufficient knowledge of the exact nature of these demands it is difficult to give the necessary help to those social workers who are faced with those problems. There is, therefore, a very real need for those social workers who have regular opportunities to work with family dynamics to formulate their experience so that theoretical understanding of this subject increases. The particular challenge to community medical social workers in this respect lies in identifying some of the changes in the patterns of family interaction in response to the threat or actuality of illness and disability. Their contributions in this area cannot but have an important enriching effect on medical social work generally by extending the boundaries of its specialist contribution.

Another form of extension of the social work method, which work with the sick and the disabled in the community is likely to require, is that of group work. Because these people live in the community and their disabilities contribute to social isolation, the social group work method seems particularly appropriate to help them to become more integrated into the community. Relatively few medical social workers practise this method at present; those who will work in the community will not only need to learn what is known about it, but will also have the responsibility to identify and formulate the medico-social components within it.

Opportunities for preventive work. The concept of 'prevention' is fraught with difficulties because it presupposes definite knowledge about what is to be prevented, and by what means. The fact that it is currently fashionable in social work does not overcome this lack of certainty. Timms (1964 a) discusses the difficulties inherent in applying the concept, which originates from social medicine, to social work, and, using as his basis the elements of prevention identified by Leavell and Clark, comes to the conclusion that only the processes of early diagnosis, limitation of the disability, and of rehabilitation, are applicable to this field. Such an approach highlights the difficulties inherent in trying to differentiate between 'preventive' work and other kinds of social work because, in a very real sense, all social work contains preventive elements. It can be further argued that the better the work, the stronger its preventive aspect. This is because a skilled social work practitioner is capable of using the less obvious diagnostic material to identify a problem, and has a readier awareness of the importance of early detection for the success of the helping process. To acknowledge this truth is not incompatible with recognising that in certain contexts opportunities for establishing contact with people whose problems are at a relatively early stage and who can therefore be helped to avoid developing serious difficulties in the realm of social functioning, are greater than in others. This is particularly true of the field of general practice. For many people their sense of physical well-being acts as a barometer in relation to the climate of their personal and social environment; unfavourable changes in their lives which give rise to tension and anxiety are likely to manifest themselves at an early stage in the form of some physical symptom or disturbance in a physiological function. Social work intervention at this stage, aimed at the roots of the trouble, can prevent a great deal of future unhappiness and suffering, including at times the development of a more severe psycho-somatic illness. For such intervention to be possible and effective, however, it is essential that it should take place in a medical setting. This follows from the fact that the need to express problems in the form of physical symptoms does not arise accidentally and that people in this situation are bound to have a considerable investment in these symptoms being taken seriously and acted upon. If social work help is presented to them as an alternative to medical treatment rather than an aid to it, it is unlikely to be acceptable. Equally, any temporary increase in anxiety in the course of the client's contact with the social worker, may easily result in either an exacerbation of the original symptoms or in the onset of new ones. In either case, medical attention is of the utmost importance, and without it the scope of social work in relation to this group of clients is bound to be very restricted. The following case summary illustrates some of these points.

Mrs. D. attended her general practitioner complaining of sleeplessness, a disinterest in food, and loss of weight. She was in her late forties, very anxious and agitated, and showed all the physical signs of thyrotoxicosis. She was, therefore, referred to the nearest teaching hospital for investigations. These showed no physiological abnormality, and she was referred back to her general practitioner. When he saw her again, she seemed much worse and in an anxiety state. When asked what was worrying her, all Mrs. D. could say was that there was a constant musty smell in her home which upset her and made it impossible for her to either eat or sleep. At this point the general practitioner decided to refer her to the medical social worker. In her first interview with the patient, the medical social worker too found it difficult to obtain a coherent picture of Mrs. D.'s situation. She talked with considerable distress of the musty smell which she attributed to the fact that the neighbours in the flat below never washed their floors. She said that she had tried to get the landlord to talk to them, but that he would not take her complaints seriously. The patient also implied that neither her husband nor her teenage daughter were showing much concern for her trouble. This feeling that no-one paid attention to her was quite marked and the medical social worker saw this as an important feature in the situation. She suggested to Mrs. D. that she might see her husband, in order to get his views on the position and perhaps obtain his permission for a visit to the flat by a Health Inspector. The patient agreed to this willingly, but expressed doubt as to whether her husband would take the trouble to come. Her doubt appeared to be confirmed as he failed to keep the appointment and sent no message. The medical social worker, conscious both of Mrs. D.'s distress and the general practitioner's concern that the nature of the patient's problem be clarified without too much delay, wrote to her husband again. This time she worded her letter to him more firmly emphasising her own and the doctor's concern for his wife's condition, and saying that if he failed to keep the appointment she was offering him this time, she would assume that she had his permission to take whatever steps she considered necessary on his wife's behalf. The husband still did not come, but on the day of his appointment a telephone message was received from Mrs. D. in which she expressed thanks for all the help the medical social worker had given her, and said that all was now well again! Intrigued and puzzled, the medical social worker decided to pay Mrs. D. a home visit to find out what had happened knowing that such a step would be welcome by the patient. The visit proved most revealing. One of the first things which struck the medical social worker on arrival was the meticulous cleanliness apparent throughout the flat. This was particularly noticeable because the house was very old and in a bad state of repair, so that a lot of dust came in through the gaps in the windows and doors. This meant that in addition to working several hours daily in the early morning and again in the evenings as an office cleaner, Mrs. D. was spending a great deal of her time on housework in her own home. In fact, her life seemed to consist of little else than cleaning and polishing. The patient's account of how her problem had come to an end was also most revealing. According to her, the medical social worker's second letter to her husband made him take her worry seriously for the first time, as a result of which he saw the landlord and demanded that he took action over the dirty neighbours below. The landlord did this straightaway and insisted that they washed their floors and generally cleaned up their flat. After this the smell disappeared.

This rather odd story can only make sense if seen within the context of Mrs. D.'s whole life at the time of the episode. In the course of her home visit to the patient, and her subsequent contacts with Mrs. D., the medical social worker learnt a great deal which enabled her to understand both some of the factors which had contributed to Mrs. D.'s problem, and the meaning to the patient of the doctor's and her own intervention in it. Mrs. D. was going through a difficult phase of her life. Three separate, and yet interdependent, factors appeared to have played an important part in unsettling her earlier adjustment. She was going through the menopause, one aspect of which for her was a sense of regret that she had had only one child and had not used her procreative capacities more fully. Her relationship with her husband had latterly become estranged and his withdrawal from her, both in the physical and the emotional sense, had meant that she lost an important source of support and was left feeling unwanted and unappreciated. Her only daughter was in the midst of her adolescent conflicts, as a result of which she too was absent from home a great deal, and when at home, treated her mother in a way which was distressing and undermining. The patient's way of trying to deal with her misery was to make herself increasingly busy, so as not to have time or strength to think—hence her taking the two part-time jobs as an office cleaner—and her excessive standards at home. This solution provided her with only partial and temporary relief, and in the long run only established a vicious circle. The harder she worked and the more tired she was, the more negatives she tended to read into her husband's and her daughter's behaviour towards her. Her own inability to respond to them made them in turn more inconsiderate and less anxious to seek her company. In addition, her hours of work necessitated her ceasing some of her previous social activities, such as morning sessions over cups of tea with her neighbours and friends, and occasional trips to the cinema. Finally, the combination of sheer physical exhaustion with emotional distress over a period of time led to the development of both physical symptoms and a neurotic type of behaviour. Had these not been recognised as serious manifestations of some underlying unhappiness and acted upon promptly, they would in all probability have led to a much more complete breakdown, and one which might have proved beyond repair. In the circumstances, things began to improve as quickly as they had gone downhill. With a little assistance from the medical social worker, some communication between Mrs. D. and her husband was re-established, and they began facing jointly, and therefore more successfully, the difficulties stemming from their daughter's adolescence. As her unhappiness subsided and she became more able to enjoy life again, Mrs. D. no longer needed to work herself so hard, and this in turn had beneficial results on her health. Throughout the period of her contact with Mrs. D. the medical social worker was in regular touch with the general practitioner, and the successful outcome of the case was influenced to a large extent by the close partnership between them.

If one accepts the criterion of a close collaboration between a medical practitioner and a social worker as an essential characteristic of preventive work with certain groups of individuals and families in the community, then this would seem an appropriate area for participation by medical social workers. It is one in which they are more likely to have a specialist contribution to make than, for example, in working with, so called, 'problem families'. The use of medical social workers in this latter type of work can be understood in the light of the overall shortage of trained social workers and the emphasis on professional social work expertise taking precedence over attention to the nature of specialisation. In the long run, however, a rational and economic deployment of resources, particularly as these will remain in short supply, will necessitate medical social workers being used in the most strategic places. These are likely to be where they can practise medical social work, and this will always require opportunities for close collaboration and ongoing communication with members of the medical profession. Lest this assertion is seen as too dogmatic and extreme, it is important to underline that it refers to the practice of medical social work, and not to the various other activities, such as administration, staff consultation, and supervision in which medical social workers engage. Their participation in these areas is equally important and needed in the community, and more specific reference to these activities will be made in the following chapter.

4
Other aspects of medical social work

Range of other work

While the central function of any profession is to provide direct service to those in need, preoccupation with this cannot be exclusive if professional responsibilities are to be carried out. There are always aspects of the cumulative experience of a profession which need to be shared with others in order that the maximum use of that experience can be made. Caplan's (1964) notion of the responsibilities of mental health workers towards providing the appropriate guidance and training for 'caretakers' in the community is one reflection of this. Equally, the value of putting to use knowledge and experience derived from other fields is demonstrated by the increasing application in the social services of various management concepts identified and tested in industry. If the validity of such mutual sharing is accepted, then it follows that social workers too have a responsibility for helping others to use in their work those aspects of social work experience which are relevant to them. In medical social work the importance of this type of contribution is further enhanced by the fact that it constitutes a small part of the activities of the health field as a whole. Therefore, its full effectiveness is dependent on its 'diffusion' through others (Bartlett, 1962 and 1963).

In addition, any profession has the responsibility of promoting the standards of work carried out by its members and the growth of knowledge which forms the basis of what is done. This responsibility manifests itself in educational activities of various kinds, in attempts to generalise from particular experiences, and in research.

It can thus be seen that these other functions cover quite an extensive range. In medical social work they can be best discussed under various headings.

Promotion of expertise and efficiency

Medical social workers in this country, like their colleagues from other fields, have in the past, been handicapped by the lack of provision for more advanced study in the various aspects of social work during the period following qualification. Opportunities for this were until recently extremely limited, and even now they are sadly inadequate. In the profession, however, there has always been a degree of recognition of the importance of ongoing development following training, and this has taken the form of various activities. These included a variety of study days, specialised seminars, and refresher courses on the different aspects of medical social work, such as the latest developments in social casework, in administrative thinking, and in supervision of both students and staff (Ziman, 1963). The Summer School organised by the Training Department of the Institute of Medical Social Workers on the application of dynamic psychology and learning theory to casework and supervision which first took place in 1961, has become an annual event as a result of continued demand for this type of opportunity for study. In addition to the various study courses which are concerned with issues of general interest to medical social workers, there has been a growing tendency within the profession for groups with specialist interests to form. Examples of such groupings are: the paediatric and geriatric groups, and, more recently, medical social workers employed by local authorities, and of those engaged in the teaching of medical students. Within these specialist sections, issues of common interest and concern are examined, and a great deal of learning by individual members from each other's experience takes place. Another important activity with a strong educational component is the Professional Conference which is held annually or bi-annually. This provides an important opportunity for the members to examine and review their own practice in the light of developments elsewhere.

From the earliest days of their existence, medical social workers have always numbered among their members a few individuals whose broad interest and intellectual capacity, coupled with personal dynamism, has enabled them to make an impact on the thinking of the profession and exercise an influence upon the direction in which it was going. This was of paramount importance in counteracting the feelings of frustration and apathy which the unequal struggle for recognition tended to engender in some of the hospital medical social workers. Acknowledgement of the contribution of these individuals and of its importance to the life of the profession as a whole is not incompatible, however, with the acceptance of another, and far less satisfactory reality. On the whole, medical social workers have been slow in looking beyond their work with individual patients, and their contributions to the fund of knowledge and experience within the profession through the medium of the written word have failed to do justice to their knowledge which would have been valuable to share with others. This fact is brought out clearly by Timms (1964 b) in his comparison of the number of articles and other written material contributed over a certain period of time by psychiatric and medical social workers respectively. The fact that an unfavourable comparison in this respect is likely to be confined to psychiatric social work, and that the position may be different in relation to the other social work groups, is no ground for complacency for medical social workers, considering both the poverty of achievement in the other fields and their own longer history and tradition as a profession.

In the field of research, with the exception of the three surveys on medical social work (Rees, 1941; *Report of the Survey Committee*, 1953; Moon and Slack, 1965) to which reference will be made later, activity on the part of individual medical social workers has been limited. It is significant, for instance, that the few contributions by social workers in this country to the subject of psycho-somatic illness, have all been made by psychiatric social workers (Goldberg, 1958; Brueton, 1962 and Westmacott, 1961). With a very few exceptions indeed (Beck, 1947; Collins, 1965; Goldwyn, 1966) participation by medical social workers in research has taken the form of assisting in various pieces of medical research. In these, their contribution was usually of a very subsidiary nature and could not be regarded as independent research work in any sense of the word. Latterly, there has been some evidence of an increased interest in research among medical social workers, the main contributions coming from the field of general practice (Collins, 1965; Fairbairn, 1966). It must be hoped that this trend will continue and will embrace other aspects of medical social work practice, such as work in hospitals and local authorities. However real the past disadvantages to the profession have been as a result of a reluctance to conceptualise, as far as its future is concerned, this is likely to be a matter of either survival or extinction. As general standards of training and practice in social work rise, so the demands which will be made on the various specialisms within it will also rise and they will be required to justify their continued existence by their contribution.

An area in which the failure by medical social workers to communicate effectively the nature of their particular contribution to medical care has had obviously harmful results for the image of medical social work, is that of relationships with doctors and nurses. Considering the extent of the difficulties in this respect which medical social workers have experienced from the outset, one is struck by the inadequacy of the efforts aimed at improving the situation. Attempts to achieve this have tended to be either at the fieldwork level in contacts between individual medical social workers and individual doctors or ward sisters over particular patients, or, at the other extreme, at the level of formal meetings between representatives of the Institute and those of the Royal Colleges (*Medical Care*, 1959). However important and useful these were, they had obvious limitations. In the case of the former, as already pointed out in Chapter 2, communications which focused on specific situations in which conflict between the medical and the psycho-social aspects of patients' needs was often a major feature, were not the most conducive for the achievement of a lasting change in attitudes and understanding. Any agreements reached through the latter medium were in danger of remaining formal pronouncements without much effect on actual practice by members of either side. The media which appear not to have been used sufficiently were those of regular group contacts between medical social workers and their other colleagues based on the actual work setting, e.g. hospital, local authority department, or group practice, and of writing about medical social work in the medical and nursing journals. These would ensure that the medical social workers' point of view about various aspects of care of sick and disabled people would be communicated to a cross section of the medical and the nursing professions.

The efficiency of any kind of work is dependent not only on the expertise of the persons who carry it out but also on the organisational framework within which it takes place. It has almost become a cliché to say that where more than two people are employed there is a need for an administrative system for the making and execution of policy, but the truth of this cannot be denied. Social workers in all fields have frequently been accused of failing to appreciate this sufficiently, or, at any rate, to accept its implications (Warham, 1967). Medical social workers have been no exception; in fact, there may be some validity in thinking that their location in the complex organisational setting of hospitals has been used by some as an excuse for not giving

73

sufficient attention to the administrative aspects of their own jobs. This was bound to have unsatisfactory effects on their work when one considers the various decisions of an administrative kind which have to be made in every medical social work department of a hospital. Decisions about the distribution of work among members of the department alone entail such considerations as the relationship between the size of caseloads in the different units and the nature and extent of the demands these make on professional time and skills. Given the reality of shortage of medical social work resources, both the nature of priorities in utilising these and the means by which these are communicated from the department to others within the hospital concerned, need to be carefully thought out. The personal nature of the help given to patients through social casework and the difficulties inherent in assessing its quality, are not a sufficient excuse for the head of the department to fail to devise ways by which she can ensure that the standard of the service offered does not fall below a certain minimum, and that members of her staff have the necessary encouragement and help to raise it to the level of their capacities.

In some aspects of 'staff management' medical social workers were ahead of their colleagues in the other fields. This is particularly true of staff supervision which was soon recognised as an important means of enabling newly qualified workers to meet the demands of their first post (Hanson, 1957; Moon, 1958). It is true that there was a certain lack of clarity about the purpose of this type of supervision and of what was entailed for both the worker and the supervisor. A particular confusion, not uncommon at one stage, was the failure to differentiate sufficiently between staff and student supervision. As a result, staff supervision was viewed excessively in educational terms, and insufficient emphasis was given to its administrative nature, namely ensuring that the required work was done and done well. Much of the confusion was gradually dispersed as a result of a number of seminars and discussions on the subject of staff supervision which enabled it to be seen more appropriately and realistically (Ziman, 1963).

In addition to staff supervision, such channels of communication within the medical social work department as regular staff meetings, were commonly accepted, and served a useful purpose in allowing for exchange of opinion and for shared decisions.

It is probably true to say that the weakest aspect of administration of medical social work services in the past has been in relation to these policies which, because they affected different departments in the hospital, called for negotiation. Many medical social workers' difficulties in this respect were a reflection of the position which was discussed at some length in Chapter 2, namely their insecure position within the hospital structure and their reluctance to bring conflicts into the open. Difficulties in implementing certain policies because they were known to be unpopular with some other sections in the hospital, have been a very real problem in the life of the profession since its early days. Their frustrating and demoralising effects were increased by the fact that they were seen and felt to be contraventions of what was regarded as right by the profession.

The dilemma can be seen clearly by looking at the three surveys into medical social workers' functions which were published in 1941, 1953, and 1964 respectively. The first of these, by H. Rees, examined the current work of almoners and made recommendations about their post-war functions. A strong and well argued plea was made for increasing the social work component of almoners' jobs and for reducing routine duties which could be performed by others than trained medical social workers. One of the purposes of the second survey, undertaken by a specially appointed committee under the chairmanship of A. D. Kelly, was to examine the extent to which the recommendations of the first survey had been carried out. The picture revealed was a depressing one : in a large number of almoners' departments such non-social work duties as provision of surgical appliances, and ordering of transport were being carried out, and in general, much time was spent on isolated and ad hoc activities which were not a part of a considered social work plan. The purpose and scope of the third survey by M. Moon with the assistance of K. M. Slack, was somewhat different in that it was concerned with the experience of a group of newly qualified medical social workers during the first two years of work. Nevertheless, the material they supplied was very enlightening with regard to the activities carried out in a large number of departments of medical social work in the country. It showed, among other findings, that in some of these between one-half and one-third of the medical social workers' time was being spent on work which could be carried out by people without professional training. In view of such a situation, it is hardly surprising that a good deal of disillusionment and frustration was found to exist among the newly qualified medical social workers, with resentment towards both their training for giving them an unattainable vision of the work, and towards their superiors for expecting them to acquiesce in the actual reality (for a discussion of this see: Butrym, 1966; Spencer, 1966). It is premature, as yet, to attempt an assessment of the effects on the profession of the Moon Report but there are indications that its findings have been taken to heart by many and will lead to more determined action than in the past to change things. The likelihood of this is further increased by the fact that such developments as the increasing demand for medical social workers by local authorities are bound to make the shortage of these workers for hospital employment even more acute and so will intensify the need to use their services more economically and more selectively. In general, the expansion of medical social work into the Health and Welfare Departments of local authorities is likely to make members of the profession more 'administratively conscious', and this is bound to have beneficial results on the effectiveness of their services in any setting.

Such a widening of its terms of reference is also likely to result in more men being attracted to medical social work. In the past, the profession has consisted almost exclusively of women, a fact closely associated with the "lady almoner" image of medical social work in its early days, which has persisted surprisingly long after it had ceased to be appropriate. The expanding nature of medical social work, in particular its opportunities in the community field, should offer men interested in social work with the sick and the disabled the necessary challenge and career opportunities which were lacking before.

Consultation

As the term 'consultation' is used in different contexts, it seems important to clarify at the outset its meaning in social work. Very briefly, the purpose of the activity is to enable another person who is faced with a perplexing work situation to deal with it with a greater understanding and ease. The purpose is achieved through sharing with the other one's own professional understanding which bears on the problem rather than by taking over the problem oneself. The range of situations calling for this type of participation by a medical social worker are many. Those who can benefit from it cover all those whose concern for people who are either sick themselves or have a sick member in the family brings them into situations where social work knowledge and skills are relevant. The following few examples will illustrate the range:

A ward sister who was very concerned about the difficult behaviour of a patient in relation to the special diet which his illness necessitated, was anxious to discuss with the medical social worker possible reasons why his aggression was confined to this one aspect of his hospital care. The medical social worker was able to show that to this man the restriction of food carried particularly depriving implications. In addition to this emotional factor, the particular type of diet was alien to him culturally and carried associations which were not easily acceptable. This understanding of the nature of her patient's difficulties, made it possible for the ward sister both to achieve certain modifications in his diet and to provide him with a number of compensations for the deprivation.

A child care officer was faced with a dilemma in relation to the request of a dying mother to see her young child with whom she had no contact for several years and who was in the care of the children's department. She relied heavily on the medical social worker for gaining an understanding of the sick woman's condition, its manifestations, and the degree of her ability to communicate, and was able then to assess the likely effects of this on the child. Also, as this particular child care officer had no previous experience in helping a child to face the serious illness or death of a parent, the medical social worker was able to help her considerably in this difficult task.

A young doctor who had been told by a woman in the out-patients department a horrific story about her war-time experiences was anxious to have the medical social worker's reactions to it to help him assess its credibility and meaning. Having decided that she was seriously disturbed emotionally, he further sought the worker's assistance in effecting a satisfactory referral to a psychiatrist.

A home help who was working for an old lady was very distressed and angry when the client insinuated that she had taken some money off the mantelpiece. She needed a good deal of clarification and support from the local authority medical social worker to help her to realise that the old lady was both forgetful and tended to lack trust in others and that, therefore, her perseverance with her was likely to have beneficial effects on the old lady, by no means confined to domestic work.

It would seem that the scope in medical social work for offering consultative help to various kinds of colleagues and other members of the community is considerable, and it is equally clear that the opportunities for this are being under-employed at present. One reason for this is that work of this nature calls for a high degree of expertise in one's own field, and for confidence in the value of what one has to offer. The fact that social work is a relatively new profession, and that, on the whole, its recognition in our society is both recent and tenuous, has been, and still remains, an important obstacle. There are grounds for thinking, however, that a good deal more consultation is carried out by medical social workers than is openly acknowledged. The effects of this 'modesty' are the absence of a sufficient number of accounts of the type of situations in which this form of professional contribution is called for, and which could serve as a basis for a more conceptualised view of it. This leads to a self-perpetuating situation in which the absence of formulations about consultation prevents effective teaching of this method of work, and the fact that people were not taught it in training makes them lack the confidence to practise it.

Education

There is a long-standing tradition in medical social work of accepting responsibility for the education of its future practitioners. The Institute of Medical Social Workers has had its own training school for many years, and this has meant that a number of practising medical social workers were involved in the educational programme both as tutors and supervisors. In addition, placements have always been provided in hospital medical social work departments for students taking the various basic social science courses at universities. In more recent years two other categories of student have been offered fieldwork experience by medical social workers: students from university courses providing training in social work, including students who intend to enter the field of medical social work and those whose choice lies in one of the other fields, and students from the Certificate in Social Work Courses (for a useful discussion of student supervision see: Young, 1967).

Medical social workers have also participated for some time in the training of medical and nursing students. The extent and nature of their contribution depends on the importance attached by a particular School to the social science component in the curriculum. The failure in many Schools, particularly Schools of Medicine, to give sufficient priority (if any) to such subjects as psychology, sociology, and social administration, imposes very real limitations on the role which the medical social worker can play in helping future doctors and nurses to be more aware of the individual and family needs of their patients, and of the existing resources for meeting these. Another frustrating aspect to the participation by medical social workers in teaching medical and nursing students has at times been the failure of those responsible for the planning of the teaching to bring them in at the planning stage. Instead, not infrequently, medical social workers are presented with a *fait accompli* in relation not only to the amount of time allocated to them but also to the content and method of the teaching which is expected of them. No teacher can offer of his best in these circumstances.

In spite of these limitations and frustrations, a number of medical social workers have developed considerable experience in this field of teaching, and its cumulative value is likely to be considerable both to their colleagues and to those who are responsible for making medical and nursing education more applicable to the demands of the present day.

Another, and a more recent, field of educational activity in which some medical social workers are already engaged and others are likely to be in future, is that of the local authorities' staff development programmes. Local Authorities are now paying increasing attention to the improvement of the personal services offered by their fieldwork staff. Posts of 'Staff Training Officer' have been introduced by a number of the authorities, and medical social workers have been appointed to several of them. The educational component of these posts is clearly very considerable, and they call for a great deal of adaptation of some of the more conventional teaching methods as well as for the introduction of new ones.

To complete the picture of the range of medical social

workers' involvement in the education of both future fellow social workers and of members of the other 'helping professions', reference must be made to the fact that a number of them teach in academic as well as in the field settings. Although the number of medical social workers who are lecturers at universities or tutors at colleges of further education, is not large, they probably form the next largest group after psychiatric social workers, of social workers so employed.

Social action

A number of the early almoners were true pioneers, instrumental in effecting various changes in the interests of their patients both within their own hospitals and outside. In later years the spirit of social reform within medical social work weakened. This happened to a large extent as a result of the problems encountered in the practice of social work within hospitals. These led to a desire to avoid conflict at all cost and also resulted in a more 'inward looking' attitude on the part of the profession which has come under criticism on a number of occasions.

It is probably true to say that, in the field of social action, medical social workers have been more effective in their response to the various requests for their opinion than in either initiating social action on their own, or in feeding back information from their daily contacts with patients on the impact of the various existing services on the sick and their families. Examples of the former type of contribution are many and include evidence submitted to the various Government working parties and committees, such as the Percy Committee on Rehabilitation, the Jamieson Committee on Health Visiting, the Younghusband Working Party on Social Workers in the Local Authority Health and Welfare Services, the Heywood Committee on Research in the Social Sciences, and most recently, to the Royal Commission on Medical Education and the Seebohm Committee on Local Authority Personal Social Services.

In some ways, medical social workers' membership of various committees at both national and local level, can be seen as a form of social action. On these committees they have the opportunity to put forward and make known the needs and the problems of the sick and disabled which come to their notice in the course of their work. The range of the various social service committees on which individual medical social workers serve is considerable, and no attempt can be made here to list anything like a representative selection. For the purpose of illustration, however, those on which medical social workers are usually *ex officio* are the Disablement Resettlement Committees and many of the local Councils of Social Service.

One obvious reason for which medical social workers, together with majority of their social work colleagues, have been relatively ineffectual in bringing to public notice the deficiences of the existing services, has been their relative insignificance in society owing to both small numbers and lack of standing. One of the most compelling motives for the various separate groups of social workers in currently considering an amalgamation and the formation of a united association of social workers, is the realisation of the gains which are bound to accrue from an increase in numbers and resources.

Professional association

Several references were made in this and in the preceding chapters to the Institute of Medical Social Workers—the professional association of this group of social workers—and no account of medical social work in Britain can be complete without some mention of the part which it has played in the development of the profession. It is the oldest professional social work association in this country, having been established in 1903 as the Hospital Almoners' Association. It was the first to appoint a full time secretary in the 1930s. For many years now it has kept a register of qualified medical social workers which has been recognised for salary negotiation purposes since the outset of the National Health Service. The effects of this on standards of practice are obvious: together with the Association of Psychiatric Social Workers, the Institute was the only association of social workers in this country whose total membership was made up of workers with an accepted professional qualification. The Institute has also initiated various important steps for the development of the profession in terms of its ability to serve the sick. It has taken the initiative on many occasions in organising study projects, conferences, and other educational activities, and has sponsored all the three Surveys into the functions of medical social workers which were discussed earlier. In addition, it has been the essential channel for submitting the evidence to the various Government committees of enquiry listed above.

As well as fulfilling all these functions, the Institute has acted consistently as a guide to the profession on a number of issues of current concern. Three recent examples of this are the leaflets it has published on teaching of medical students, on the organisation of medical social work departments in hospitals, and on the contribution of medical social workers to the Local Authority health and welfare services (1965 a and b, 1966).

Another very important activity which has been carried out by medical social workers' professional association since 1949 has been the publication of a monthly journal. This has served as an important forum for professional communication between the members, and a useful educational organ through which the ideas and practice of the more advanced among them could be made available to the rest. Also, some of the developments in medicine particularly relevant to social work were reported and commented upon by various specialists. The quality of the different contributions has obviously varied, but on the whole there has been a steady improvement over the years, and for those who are willing to make use of it, the *Journal of Medical Social Work* (previously *The*

Almoner) usually contains a good deal of material for thought.

Possibly, the greatest single contribution (because all the others depend on it) the Institute has made to the development of medical social work is that of giving the profession a sense of identity, particularly in the earlier days when social work was not conceived as having an entity of its own, and the different groups of social workers were considered and considered themselves as separate professions. This enabled the individual members of the medical social work profession to carry their burdens in the knowledge that they were shared with colleagues all over the country, and provided the basis for a shared philosophy and a common loyalty which are indispensable to any profession.

The authority and prestige of this professional association has not prevented it from recognising at an early stage of the 'generic' developments in social work the likely advantages if all social workers were organised in one unified profession. Although the Institute is one of the present separate associations which probably has most to lose from an amalgamation, it seems certain that the majority of its membership will shortly decide in favour of joining with the other social work groups now represented at the Standing Conference of Organisations of Social Workers. When the unification comes, it must be hoped that the advantages inherent in it can be combined with a due recognition of the importance of preserving and encouraging specialist interests within social work. Otherwise, it is difficult to envisage real progress in the growth of a body of social work knowledge without which the future of social work cannot look very promising.

5
Guide to the literature

It will be evident from the preceding chapters that the nature of medical social work specialisation derives from its concern with the problems of the sick and the disabled, and from the need for a partnership with other professions, particularly medicine, engaged in the treatment and care of this group. In order to understand medical social work, it is necessary to give attention to: the psychology and sociology of illness; the characteristics of the various health institutions, including the different professions involved in the provision of medical care; and the many issues inherent in establishing medical social work practice appropriate both to the needs of the consumers and the resources available within the profession. Before some of the literature on these various topics is reviewed a few of the main textbooks on social work in general should be referred to, in order that the specialism of medical social work can be seen in its proper context.

Social casework

The following three publications provide between them a very comprehensive view of the subject: Helen Perlman, *Social Casework: a Problem-solving Process* (University of Chicago Press, 1957); Noel Timms, *Social Casework: Principles and Practice* (London: Routledge and Kegan Paul,

1964), and Florence Hollis, *Casework: a Psycho-Social Therapy* (New York: Random House, 1964). These three works are in many ways complementary: Perlman provides the more comprehensive framework but at the expense of a more detailed discussion of particular features; Timms deals with a number of selected aspects and considers these at some depth, its focus being upon the underlying principles rather than on techniques of practice; Hollis concerns herself more directly with the latter and her discussion of the 'helping procedures' employed by social caseworkers constitutes a particularly useful contribution. In addition, the three authors put somewhat different emphasis on the nature of social work activity: Perlman views it as predominantly 'a problem solving process'; to Timms it is a way of promoting the aims of particular social agencies; whilst Hollis sees it as a treatment process. Although these viewpoints are not basically incompatible, they nevertheless represent different approaches to the role of social work and thus both reflect and contribute towards the lack of a clear consensus of opinion among social workers as to their exact terms of reference.

General on medical social work

Harriett Bartlett, the American author, has been the most prolific writer and the most original contributor to the subject. Her first book *Some Aspects of Social Casework in a Medical Setting* (New York: National Association of Social Workers, 1940), is a very useful and imaginative account of the needs which clients in the medical setting present, and of the nature of the medical social worker's contribution towards meeting them. Her two more recent companion volumes, *Analyzing Social Work Practice by Fields* and *Social Work Practice in the Health Field* (both New York: National Association of Social Workers, 1961) make an important contribution towards our understanding of the relationship between the 'generic' and the 'specialist' elements in medical social work. Two later articles by this author, 'Frontiers of Medical Social Work' (*The Almoner* Vol. XV, September, 1962), and 'The Widening Scope of Hospital Medical Social Work' (*Social Casework* Vol. XIIV, January, 1963), are concerned with the evolution of medical social work practice in the light of the various changes in the field of medical treatment and care, and developments in social work thinking.

In this country the contributions by Jean Snelling have been particularly valuable and her article 'Social Work within Medical Care' (*The Almoner* Vol. XV, June, 1962), needs to be especially mentioned in this section. Equally reference must be made to the chapter on Medical Social Work in the already mentioned book *Social Casework* by Noel Timms in which will be found a very perceptive account of many of the characteristics of social work within medical care.

The collection of readings edited by Dora Goldstine, *Readings in the Theory and Practice of Medical Social Work* (University of Chicago Press, 1954), is also very useful, and contains contributions on problems of working with particular groups of patients, of meeting problems of dependency in sick people, and on what is entailed in 'Teamwork'.

Psychology and sociology of illness

This is a wide area, and there is so much relevant literature, that the task of providing a useful selection of references is particularly difficult.

Both ego psychology and the psychology of crisis situations, have an important contribution to make towards our understanding of psychological reactions to illness and disability. Here, a number of articles in the two collections edited by H. J. Parad, *Ego Psychology and Dynamic Casework, Part I.* (New York: Family Service Association of America, 1960) and *Crisis Intervention: Selected Readings* (New York: Family Service Association of America, 1965) are of considerable value. Papers by the following authors deal helpfully with the various aspects of the psychology of illness: B. Ackner, 'Stress and Disease' (*The Almoner*, Vol. XI, February, 1958); C. G. Babcock 'Inner Stress in Illness and Disability' in *Ego Oriented Casework: Problems and Perspectives*, eds. H. J. Parad and R. R. Miller (New York: Family Service Association of America); Sir G. H. Godber, 'Social Factors in Medicine' (*Medical Social Work* Vol. XVIII, May, 1965); J. M. Snelling, 'Grief reactions in the field of Medical Social Work' (*Case Conference*, December, 1955); M. S. Spelman and P. Ley, 'Psychological Reactions to Illness and Hospitalisation in a Group of Medical Inpatients' (*Social Work*, January, 1966); A. Storr, 'The Psychological Effects of Physical Illness' (*The Almoner* Vol. XIII, March, 1960).

With regard to psychosomatic illness in the more restricted sense of the term, the World Health Organisation Monograph *Psychosomatic Disorders* (1964) contains a very useful discussion on the meaning of the concept 'psychosomatic'. Works by F. Alexander, *Psychosomatic Medicine* (London: Allen & Unwin, 1952), and E. Weiss and O. S. English, *Psychosomatic Medicine* (New York: W. B. Saunders, 1957) are standard textbooks on the subject. In addition the book by M. Balint, *The Doctor, his Patient and the Illness* (London: Pitman Medical Publishing Co., 1957) has a value which is by no means confined to the field of general medical practice for which it is primarily intended. The account by E. M. Goldberg, of a study of a group of young men suffering from duodenal ulcers, and of their families, *Family Influences and Psychosomatic Illness* (London: Tavistock Publications, 1958) provides some useful and interesting information on the socio-psychological environment of these patients.

No true understanding of illness and of its implications (including the psychological effects) for the patient and his family is possible without a sound grasp of the relevant physiological factors. Yet it is not easy for someone without medical training to acquire this. Attention is drawn to this dilemma for two reasons: firstly to emphasise for all intending medical social workers the importance of studying both the normal physiology of the human organism and the various disease processes; and secondly, to explain the failure to include particular medical textbooks in suggestions for reading. There are, however, a large number of these and the matter of choice is so individual that it seems wiser to leave the selection to the students themselves. An article which merits specific recommendation on the grounds that it provides such a clear and convincing justification for the relevance of physiological knowledge to social work is that by H. M. Margolis 'The Biodynamic Point of View in Medicine' (*Social Casework* Vol. XXX, January, 1949).

Books in which a number of social and cultural factors in attitudes towards both illness and treatment are usefully considered are those—by L. Saunders, *Cultural Differences and Medical Care* (New York: Russell Sage Foundation, 1954); L. W. Simmons and H. H. Wolff, *Social Science in Medicine* (New York: Russell Sage Foundation, 1954); and M. W. Susser and W. Watson, *Sociology in Medicine* (London: Oxford University Press, 1963).

Sociology of the health institutions

In recent years there has been a considerable growth in literature on the various sociological aspects of medical care, but in spite of this there are still considerable gaps in some areas. One of these is the absence of studies of general hospitals on lines similar to those of mental hospitals. The study by T. Ferguson and A. N. Macphail, *Hospital and Community* (London: Oxford University Press, 1954) is a useful contribution. Others which deserve mention in this context are: A. Cartwright, *Human Relations and Hospital Care* (London: Routledge and Kegan Paul, 1964); C. Sofer, 'Reactions to Administrative Change: A Study of Staff Relations in three British Hospitals' (*Human Relations* Vol. VIII, 1955). There are also some useful articles on various aspects of medical care in H. J. McLachlan, ed. *Problems and*

G

Progress in Medical Care (London : Oxford University Press, 1964).

For the reader who is interested in seeing the current issues in medical treatment and care against a broader administrative and historical background, the following works can be recommended: B. Abel-Smith, 'Paying the Family Doctor' (*Medical Care* Vol. I, No. 1, 1963), and *The Hospitals, 1800-1948: A Study in Social Administration in England and Wales* (London: Heinemann, 1964); A. Lindsey, *Socialized Medicine in England and Wales: The National Health Service, 1948–61* (University of North Carolina Press, 1962); T. McKeown, *Medicine in Modern Society* (London: Allen & Unwin, 1965); R. Stevens, 'Hospital Administration—The Status Quo' (*Medical Care* Vol. II, No. 4, 1964); 'Care in the Community—A Symposium' (*Social Work*, April and July, 1965); M. Jefferys, *An Anatomy of Social Welfare Services* (London: Michael Joseph, 1965); and R. W. Revans, *Standards for Morale: Cause and Effect in Hospital* (London: Oxford University Press, 1966).

Several studies are available of the various health professions in terms of their status in society, the nature of role conflicts experienced by their members and of their problems in collaborating with others. Two studies of the nursing profession are of considerable interest: B. Abel-Smith, *A History of the Nursing Profession* (London: Heinemann, 1960), and I. E. P. Menzies, 'A Case Study in the Functioning of Social Systems as a Defence against Anxiety' (*Human Relations* Vol. XIII, May, 1960). The following studies of doctors should have particular mention: H. S. Becker *et al.*, *Boys in White: Student Culture in Medical School* (University of Chicago Press, 1963); E. G. Jaco ed., *Patients, Physicians and Illness* (Glencoe: The Free Press, 1958); and R. K. Merton, G. G. Reader and P. L. Kendall, eds. *The Student Physician—Introductory Studies in the Sociology of Medical Education* (Harvard University Press, 1957). Articles which are concerned with the role and functions of medical social workers, and which are to be recommended are the following: J. M. Snelling, 'The Impact of the Hospital on its Social Worker' (*The Almoner* Vol. XV, December, 1962); S. D. King, 'Communication and Collaboration' (*The Almoner* Vol. XVI, June, 1963); N. Timms, 'Communication and Collaboration' (*The Almoner* Vol. XVI, June, 1963); and K. Jones, 'Society as the Client' (*Medical Social Work* Vol. XIX, June, 1966 (Conference Supplement).

Various aspects of medical social work practice

Social work with the sick and the disabled. In addition to the references already mentioned in the general section, there are a number of articles by medical social workers and others on various aspects of social work with patients and relatives. Only a small proportion of these could be selected for particular mention here, and in choosing them an effort was made to cover as wide a range of topics of concern to medical social workers as possible: M. Birley, 'Terminal Care' (*The Almoner* Vol. XIII, June, 1960); M. E. Burnett, 'Some Thoughts about Dying' (*The Almoner* Vol. XI, October, 1958); M. Brueton, 'Casework with Asthmatic Children' (*Case Conference* Vol. IX, September, 1962), and 'An Experiment in Groupwork with Adolescent Skin Patients' (*The Almoner* Vol. XVI, March, 1963); R. Challenger, 'Relatives' (*The Almoner* Vol. XVII, July, 1964); P. St. C. Corby, 'The Almoner's Contribution to the Prevention of Mental Ill-Health' (*The Almoner* Vol. XIII, March, 1960); M. P. Daniel, 'Casework with Sick Children and their Parents' (*Case Conference* Vol. XI, February, 1964); C. Fudge, 'Working with Parents of Hydrocephalic Children' (*The Almoner* Vol. XV, December, 1962); H. Lambrick, 'Communication with the Patient' (*The Almoner* Vol. XV, October, 1962); J. G. Ledingham, D. H. Ziman and Z. T. Butrym, 'Case Study Mrs. A.' (*The Almoner* Vol. XV, November, 1962); A. H. Parks, 'Short Term Casework in a Medical Setting' (*Social Work* (U.S.A.), October, 1963); and A. Hartshorn, 'Psychological Aspects of "Stroke" Illness' (*Medical Social Work* Vol. XIX, March, 1967, and 'The Role of the Social Worker in the Treatment of "Stroke" Illness' (*Medical Social Work* Vol. XX, April, 1967).

Relationship with other workers. For reasons which were discussed at some length in the previous chapters, medical social workers have always given a good deal of their attention to the two issues of their function within the field of medical care and their relationship with other health workers, in particular with doctors and nurses. Not surprisingly therefore, much of medical social work literature is also concerned with these topics.

The three Surveys on medical social workers' functions which have been carried out by the medical social work profession makes interesting and informative reading: H. E. Rees, *A Survey* (London: Hospital Almoners' Association, 1941); 'Report of the Survey Committee' (*The Almoner* Vol. VI, May, 1953); and E. M. Moon and K. M. Slack, *The First Two Years: a Study of the Work Experience of some Newly Qualified Medical Social Workers* (London: The Institute of Medical Social Workers, 1965). All three Reports gave rise to much discussion within the profession after they were published, and a picture of the reactions to the last one of these will be obtained from the Report of the Proceedings of the Professional Conference of the Institute of Medical Social Workers (*Medical Social Work* Vol. XIX, June, 1966).

A. Hartshorn has written a useful article on the place of medical social work in hospital and the issues inherent in practice in that setting, 'Social Work and the Hospital' (*The Almoner* Vol. XVI, October, 1963).

The need for a more economic use of medical social workers' professional resources in hospital work has attracted a good deal of attention in recent years, and the following contributions give some idea of the issues involved: P. Lewis, 'Widening Our Horizons—a Look at American Administration' (*The Almoner* Vol. XVII, October, 1964);

E. M. Moon, 'Making the Best Use of Trained Staff' (*The Almoner* Vol. XI, July, 1958); H. Bate, 'Selection and Training for Welfare Assistants' (*Medical Social Work* Vol. XIX, October, 1966); and A. Ullman and G. G. Kassebaum, 'Referrals and Services in a Medical Social Work Department' (*Social Service Review*, September, 1961).

Following the publication of the Younghusband Report (*Report of the Working Party on Social Workers in the Local Authority Health and Welfare Services* (London: H.M.S.O., 1959), the application of medical social work skills to work in the community has received a fair amount of attention. The following articles are of an interest in connection with this: M. Dongray, 'Social Work in General Practice' (*Case Conference* Vol. VI, June, 1959); E. Fairbairn, 'Medical Social Work and General Practice' (*Medical Social Work* Vol. XIX, July, 1966); and E. Gloyne, 'Medical Social Work Practice in Public Health' (*The Almoner* Vol. XVI, July, 1963). Joan Collins' study of the need for social work help of patients in a group general practice should also be mentioned in this context *Social Casework in a General Medical Practice* (London: Pitman Medical Publishing Co., 1965).

Medical social workers have taken part in medical education for some time. The following two articles by medical social workers and one by a doctor discuss some aspects of this educational function: J. Paterson, 'The Almoner's Contribution to Medical Teaching' (*The Almoner* Vol. III, August and September, 1950); J. McNicol, 'The role of the Almoner in the teaching of Medical Students' (*The Almoner* Vol. XI, February, 1959) and M. D. Warren, 'Social and Preventive Medicine and the Medical Social Worker' (*The Almoner* Vol. IX, June, 1956).

Research has not been given adequate attention by medical social work practitioners. A plea for change in attitudes towards it is made by M. Dennis, 'Research—Anathema or Enlightenment' (*The Almoner* Vol. XIV, August, 1961).

Problems of collaboration with others are dealt with in

the following papers: S. D. King (1963) and N. Timms (1963), mentioned above; J. Garrad, 'On the Margin of the Impossible' (*Medical Social Work* Vol. XIX, June, 1966); M. Dongray, 'Co-operation in General Practice' (*The Almoner* Vol. XV, March, 1962); E. Lemere-Long, 'Communication with other Social Services' (*The Almoner* Vol. XV, November, 1962); and E. W. Wilson and H. M. Bartlett, 'Referrals from Hospitals to Social Agencies: Some Principles and Problems' (*The Almoner* Vol. IX, June, 1956). The study of referrals from a hospital social work department to one of their area offices, published by Family Welfare Association (1962) is also of interest in relation to this topic.

Professional Competence. Medical social workers' long professional tradition, coupled with their responsibilities in training new entrants and for ensuring standards in connection with registration, has meant that the subjects of professional education and professional standards have always received a good deal of attention. The following contributions reflect these interests and their evolution over time: J. M. Snelling, 'Training for Medical Social Work' (*The Almoner* Vol. X, February, 1957); J. M. Hanson, 'The value of Supervision during my First Year as an Almoner' (*The Almoner* Vol. X, May, 1957); E. M. Moon, 'The Use of Supervision in providing a Casework Service to the Patient' (*The Almoner* Vol. XI, July, 1958); J. Garrad, 'Some Reflections on the Philosophy of Medical Social Work' (*The Almoner* Vol. XII, July, August and September, 1959); D. H. Ziman, 'The Struggle for Professional Competence' (*The Almoner* Vol. XVI, March, 1963); J. Groombridge, 'Some Observations on Professional Practice' (*The Almoner* Vol. XVI, November, 1963); F. Beck, 'On Belonging to a Profession' (*Medical Social Work* Vol. XVIII, June, 1965); and J. Garrad (1966), mentioned above.

In addition, mention must be made of the various publications of the Institute of Medical Social Workers which are issued periodically to provide guidance to their own members, and to others, on various aspects of professional function. The latest of these are *The Medical Social Worker in the Community Health and Welfare Services; Function and Organisation of a Social Work Department in a Hospital*; and *The Contribution of the Medical Social Worker to the Teaching of Medical Students* (London : Swale Press, 1965 and 1966).

Bibliography

ABEL-SMITH, B. (1960) *A History of the Nursing Profession*, London: Heinemann.

ABEL-SMITH, B. (1963) 'Paying the Family Doctor', *Medical Care*, Vol. 1, No. 1.

ABEL-SMITH, B. (1964) *The Hospitals, 1800-1948: A Study in Social Administration in England and Wales*, London: Heinemann.

ACKNER, B. (1958) 'Stress and Disease', *The Almoner*, Vol. XI. February.

ALEXANDER, F. (1952) *Psychosomatic Medicine*, London: Allen & Unwin.

BABCOCK, C. G. (1963) 'Inner Stress in Illness and Disability', *Ego Oriented Casework: Problems and Perspectives*, Parad, H. J. & Miller, R. R., eds., New York: Family Service Association of America.

BALINT, M. (1957) *The Doctor, his Patient and the Illness*, London: Pitman Medical Publishing Co.

BARTLETT, H. M. (1940) *Some Aspects of Social Casework in a Medical Setting*, New York: National Association of Social Workers.

BARTLETT, H. M. (1961 a) *Analyzing Social Work Practice by Fields*, New York: National Association of Social Workers.

BARTLETT, H. M. (1961 b) *Social Work Practice in the Health Field*, New York: National Association of Social Workers.

BARTLETT, H. M. (1962) 'Frontiers of Medical Social Work', *The Almoner*, Vol. XV. September.

BARTLETT, H. M. (1963) *The Widening Scope of Hospital Medical Social Work*, Social Casework, Vol. XLIV. January.

BATE, H. (1966) 'Selection and Training for Welfare Assistants', *Medical Social Work*, Vol. XIX. October.

BIBLIOGRAPHY

BECK, F. (1965) 'On Belonging to a Profession', *Medical Social Work*, Vol. XVIII. June.

BECK, F., GARDNER, F. V., and WITTS, L. J. (1947). 'Social Services for a Medical Ward', *British Journal of Social Medicine*.

BECKER, H. S. & others (1963) *Boys in White: Student Culture in Medical School*, University of Chicago Press.

BIRLEY, M. (1960) 'Terminal Care', *The Almoner*, Vol. XIII. June.

BRUETON, M. (1962) 'Casework with Asthmatic Children', *Case Conference*, Vol. IX. September.

BRUETON, M. (1963) 'An Experiment in Group work with Adolescent Skin Patients', *The Almoner*, Vol. XVI. March.

BURNETT, M. E. (1958) 'Some Thoughts about Dying', *The Almoner*, Vol. XI. October.

BUTRYM, Z. T. (1966 a) 'Some Implications of the "First Two Years" on Education and Practice', *Medical Social Work*, Vol. XIX. June (Conference Supplement).

BUTRYM, Z. T. (1966 b) *Study of Medical Social Work Practice in a London Hospital*, (unpublished).

CAPLAN, G. (1964) *Principles of Preventive Psychiatry*, London: Tavistock Publications.

'Care in the Community—A Symposium' (1965), *Social Work*, Vol. XXII. April & July.

CARTWRIGHT, A. (1964) *Human Relations and Hospital Care*, London: Routledge & Kegan Paul.

CHALLENGER, R. (1964) 'Relatives', *The Almoner*, Vol. XVII. July.

COHEN, P. C. (1962) 'The Impact of the Handicapped Child on the Family', *Social Casework*, Vol. XLIII. March.

COLES, R. B. (1959), 'Casework in Dermatology', *The Almoner*, Vol. XII. March.

COLLINS, J. (1965) *Social Casework in a General Medical Practice*, London: Pitman Medical Publishing Co. Ltd.

CORBY, P. ST. C. (1960) 'The Almoner's Contribution to the Precention of Mental Ill Health', *The Almoner*, Vol. XIII. March.

DANIEL, M. P. (1964) 'Casework with Sick Children and their Parents', *Case Conference*, Vol. XI. February.

DAVIS, M. M. (1963) 'What should Sociology contribute to Medicine?', *Medical Care*, Vol. 1. January-March.

DENNIS, M. (1961) 'Research—Anathema or Enlightenment?', *The Almoner*, Vol. XIV. August.

DONGRAY, M. (1959) 'Social Work in General Practice', *Case Conference*, Vol. VI. June.

DONGRAY, M. (1962) 'Co-operation in General Practice', *The Almoner*, Vol. XV. March.

EDELSTYN, G. A. & LAIRD, C. (1958) 'Certain Social Aspects of Hypophysectomy in Advanced Breast Cancer', *The Almoner*, Vol. XI. September.

FAIRBAIRN, E. (1966) 'Medical Social Work and General Practice', *Medical Social Work*, Vol. XIX. July.

FAMILY WELFARE ASSOCIATION (1962) *The Family: Patients or Clients*, London: Faith Press.

FERGUSON, T. & MACPHAIL, A. N. (1954) *Hospital and Community*, London: Oxford University Press.

FUDGE, C. (1962) 'Working with Parents of Hydrocephalic Children', *The Almoner*, Vol. XV. December.

GARRAD, J. (1959) 'Some Reflections on the Philosophy of Medical Social Work', *The Almoner*, Vol. XII July, August and September.

GARRAD, J. (1966) 'On the Margin of the Impossible', *Medical Social Work*, Vol. XIX. June.

GLOYNE, E. (1963) 'Medical Social Work Practice in Public Health', *The Almoner*, Vol. XVI. July.

GODBER, SIR G. (1965), 'Social Factors in Medicine', *Medical Work*, Vol. XVIII. May.

GOLDBERG, E. M. (1958) *Family Influences and Psychosomatic Illness*, London: Tavistock Publications Ltd.

GOLDBERG, E. M. (1966) *Welfare in the Community*, London: National Council of Social Service.

GOLDSTINE, D., ed. (1954) *Readings in the Theory and Practice of Medical Social Work*, University of Chicago Press.

GOLDWYN, M. C. (1966) 'The Social Needs of Hospital Patients', *Medical Care*, Vol. IV, No. 3.

GORER, G. (1965) *Death, Grief and Mourning in Contemporary Britain*, London: Cresset Press.

GROOMBRIDGE, J. (1963) 'Some Observations on Professional Practice', *The Almoner*, Vol. XVI. November.

GROUP FOR ADVANCEMENT OF PSYCHIATRY (1965) *Symposium No. 11: Death and Dying: Attitudes of Patient and Doctor*, New York: G.A.P.

HANSON, J. M. (1957) 'The Value of Supervision during my First Year as an Almoner', *The Almoner*, Vol. X. May.

HARTSHORN, A. (1963) 'Social Work and the Hospital', *The Almoner*, Vol. XVI. October.

HARTSHORN, A. (1967 a) 'Psychological Aspects of "Stroke" Illness', *Medical Social Work*, Vol. XIX. March.

HARTSHORN, A. (1967 b) 'The Role of the Social Worker in the Treatment of "Stroke" Illness', *Medical Social Work*, Vol. XX. April.

HEYMAN, M. M. (1961) 'Criteria for the Allocation of Cases according to Levels of Staff Skill', *Social Casebook*, Vol. XLII. July.

H.M.S.O. (1959) *Report of the Working Party on Social Workers in the Local Authority Health and Welfare Services*, London.

H.M.S.O (1965) Central Health Services Council—Standing Medical Advisory Committee : *The Standardisation of Hospital Medical Records*, London.

H.M.S.O. (1966) *Social Work and the Community: Proposals for Reorganising Local Authority Services in Scotland*. Cmnd. 3065, London.

HINTON, J. (1967) *Dying*, Harmondsworth : Penguin.

HOLLAND, W. W., GARRAD, J., BENNETT, A. E. & RHODES, P. (1966) 'A Clinical Approach to the Teaching of Social Medicine', *The Lancet*, Vol. 1, No. 7436, 5th March.

HOLLIS, F. (1964) *Casework—A Psychosocial Therapy*, New York : Random House.

HUGH-JONES, P., TANSER, A. R., & WHITBY, C. (1964), 'Patient's View of Admission to a London Teaching Hospital', *British Medical Journal*, Vol. II, 12th September.

INGLIS, B. (1966) 'Psyche submerged', *The Lancet*, Vol. II, No. 7476, 10th September.

INSTITUTE OF MEDICAL SOCIAL WORKERS (1965 a) *Function and Organisation of a Social Work Department in Hospital*, London : Swale Press.

INSTITUTE OF MEDICAL SOCIAL WORKERS (1965 b) *The Medical Social Worker in Community Health and Welfare Services*, London : Swale Press.

INSTITUTE OF MEDICAL SOCIAL WORKERS (1965) *The Contribution of the Medical Social Worker to the Teaching of Medical Students*, London : Swale Press.

JACO, E. G., ed. (1958) *Patients, Physicians, and Illness*, Glencoe : The Free Press.

JEFFERYS, M. (1965 a) *An Anatomy of Social Welfare Services: A Survey of Social Welfare Staff and their Clients in the County of Buckinghamshire*, London : Michael Joseph.

JEFFERYS, M. (1965 b) 'The Uncertain Health Visitor', *New Society*, 28th October.

JEFFERYS, M. (1966) 'Our Social Welfare Organisation—Its Strength and Weaknesses', *Medical Social Work*, Vol. XIX. July.

JONES, K. (1966) 'Society as the Client', *Medical Social Work*, Vol. XIX. June (Conference Supplement).

KING, S. D. (1963) 'Communication and Collaboration', *The Almoner*, Vol. XVI. June.

LAMBRICK, H. (1962) 'Communication with the Patient', *The Almoner*, Vol. XV. October.

LEDINGHAM, J. G., ZIMAN, D. H. & BUTRYM, Z. T. (1962) 'Case Study Mrs. A.', *The Almoner*, Vol. XV. April.

LEMERE-LONG, E. (1962) 'Communication with other Social Services', *The Almoner*, Vol. XV. November.

LEONARD, P. (1966) *Sociology in Social Work*, London: Routledge & Kegan Paul.

LEWIS, P. (1964) 'Widening our Horizons—a Look at American Administration', *The Almoner*, Vol. XVII. October.

LINDSEY, A. (1962) *Socialized Medicine in England and Wales: The National Health Service, 1948-1961*, University of North Carolina Press.

MACGUIRE, J. (1966) *From Student to Nurse, Area Nurse Training Committee*. Oxford.

MCKEOWN, T. (1965) *Medicine in Modern Society*, London: Allen & Unwin.

MCLACHLAN, H. J., ed. (1964) *Problems and Progress in Medical Care*, London: Oxford University Press.

MCNICOL, J. (1959) 'The Role of the Almoner in the Teaching of Medical Students', *The Almoner*, Vol. XI. February.

MARGOLIS, H. M. (1949) 'The biodynamic point of view in medicine, Social Casework*, Vol. XXX. January.

MEDICAL CARE: Statement by Representatives of the Physicians, Surgeons, Obstetricians and Almoners (1959), *The Almoner*, Vol. XII. June.

MENZIES, I. E. P. (1960) 'A Case Study in the Functioning of Social Systems as a Defence against Anxiety', *Human Relations*, Vol. XIII. May.

MERTON, R. K., READER, G. G. & KENDALL, P. L. eds. (1957) *The Student Physician—Introductory Studies in the Sociology of Medical Education*, Harvard University Press.

MOON, E. M. (1958) 'The Use of Supervision in providing a

Casework Service to the Patient', *The Almoner*, Vol. XI. July.

MOON, E. M. & SLACK, K. M. (1965) *The First Two Years: a Study of the Work Experience of some Newly Qualified Medical Social Workers*, London : The Institute of Medical Social Workers.

MOON, E. M. (1966) 'Making the Best Use of Trained Staff', *Medical Social Work*, Vol. XIX. October.

PARAD, H. J. ed. (1960) *Ego Psychology and Dynamic Casework —Part 1*. New York: Family Service Association of America.

PARAD, H. J., ed. (1965) *Crisis Intervention: Selected Readings*, New York: Family Service Association of America.

PARKS, A. H. (1963) 'Short term Casework in a Medical Setting', *Social Work*, (U.S.A.), October.

PARSONS, T. (1951) *The Social System*, Chapter X, Glencoe: The Free Press.

PATERSON, J. (1950) 'The Almoner's Contribution to Medical Teaching', *The Almoner*, Vol. III. August & September.

PERLMAN, H. H. (1957) *Social Casework: A Problem Solving Process*, Chicago University Press.

POTTER, R. S. J. (1966) 'Administrative and Social Work Problems of Services for the Handicapped', *Social Work*, Vol. XXIII. July.

REES, H. E. (1941) *A Survey*, London: Hospital Almoners' Association.

Report of the Survey Committee (1953) *The Almoner*, Vol. VI. May.

'Report of the Proceedings of the Professional Conference of the Institute of Medical Social Workers (1966) *Medical Social Work*, Vol. XIX. June (Conference Supplement).

REVANS, R. W. (1966) *Standards for Morale: Cause and Effect in Hospital*, London: Oxford University Press.

RODGERS, B. N. & DIXON, J. (1960) *Portrait of Social Work—A Study of Social Services in a Northern Town*, London: Oxford University Press.

—— M.S. (1964) 'General Social Workers in the Hospital', *The Almoner*, Vol. XVI. February.

SAUNDERS, L. (1954) *Cultural Differences and Medical Care*, New York: Russell Sage Foundation.

SCOTT, R. (1956) 'Edinburgh University General Practice Teaching Unit', *Journal of Medical Education*, Vol. XXXI.

SIEGEL, D. (1958) 'Social Work in the Medical Setting—An Instrument of Health', *The Almoner*, Vol. XI. April.

SIMMONS, L. W. & WOLFF, H. G. (1954) *Social Science in Medicine*, New York: Russell Sage Foundation.

SNELLING, J. M. (1955) 'Grief Reactions in the Field of Medical Social Work', *Case Conference*, Vol. II. December.

SNELLING, J. M. (1957) 'Training for Medical Social Work', *The Almoner*, Vol. X. February.

SNELLING, J. M. (1962 a), 'The Impact of the Hospital on its Social Worker', *The Almoner*, Vol. XV. December.

SNELLING, J. M. (1962 b) 'Social Work within Medical Care', *The Almoner*, Vol. XV. June.

SOFER, C. (1955) 'Reactions to Administrative Change: A Study of Staff Relations in three British Hospitals', *Human Relations*, Vol. VIII.

SPELMAN, M. S. & LEY P. (1966) 'Psychological Reactions to Illness and Hospitalisation in a Group of Medical In-patients', *Social Work*. January.

SPENCER, E. (1966) 'Some Implications (of "The First Two Years") on Education and Practice', *Medical Social Work*, Vol. XIX. June (Conference Supplement).

STEVENS, R. (1964) 'Hospital Administration—The Status Quo', *Medical Care*, Vol. II, No. 4.

STORR, A. (1960) 'The Psychological Effects of Physical Illness', *The Almoner*, Vol. XIII. March.

SUSSER, N. W. & WATSON, W. (1962) *Sociology in Medicine*, London: Oxford University Press.

TIMMS, N. (1963) 'Communication and Collaboration', *The Almoner*, Vol. XVI. June.

TIMMS, N. (1964 a) *Social Casework: Principles and Practice*, London: Routledge & Kegan Paul.

TIMMS, N. (1964 b) *Psychiatric Social Work in Great Britain 1939-1962*, London: Routledge & Kegan Paul.

TITMUSS, R. M. (1954) 'Science and the Sociology of Medical Care', *British Journal of Psychiatric Social Work*, Vol. III, No. 4.

TITMUSS, R. M. (1958) *Essays on 'the Welfare State'*, London: Allen & Unwin.

TITMUSS, R. M. (1963) 'Ethics and Economics of Medical Care', *Medical Care*, Vol. I, No. 1.

TRAVIS, G. (1961) *Chronic Disease and Disability*, University of California Press.

ULLMAN, A. and KASSEBAUM, G. G. (1961) 'Referrals and Services in a Medical Social Work Department', *Social Service Review*, September.

WARHAM, J. (1967) *An Introduction to Administration for Social Workers*, London: Routledge & Kegan Paul.

WARREN, M. D. (1960) 'Social and Preventive Medicine and the Medical Social Worker', *The Almoner*, Vol. XIII. November.

WEISS, E. & ENGLISH, O. S. (1957) *Psychosomatic Medicine*, New York: W. B. Saunders Co.

WESTMACOTT, I. (1961) 'Psychiatric Social Work in a Paediatric Setting', *Case Conference*, Vol. VIII. January.

WILLIAMS, M. (1966) 'Changing Attitudes to Death: A Survey of Contributions in Psychological Abstracts over a Thirty-year Period', *Human Relations*, Vol. XIX, No. 4.

WILSON, E. W. & BARTLETT, H. M. (1956) 'Referrals from Hospitals to Social Agencies: Some Principles and Problems', *The Almoner*, Vol. IX. June.

WINNICOTT, C. (1964) 'Casework and Agency Function', *Child Care and Social Work*, Codicote Press.

WOODWARD, J. M. (1961) 'Notes on the Role Concept in Casework with Mothers of Burned Children', *The Almoner*, Vol. XIV. May.

WORLD HEALTH ORGANISATION (1964) *Psychosomatic Disorders*, Technical Report Series, No. 275, Geneva.

YOUNG, P. (1967) *The Student and Supervision in Social Work Education*, London: Routledge & Kegan Paul.

ZIMAN, D. H. (1963) 'The Struggle for Professional Competence', *The Almoner*, Vol. XVI. March.